DRAWING

MATERIALS, TECHNIQUES, STYLES, AND PRACTICE

EDITED BY
TRENTON CAMPBELL

Britannica®
Educational Publishing
IN ASSOCIATION WITH

ROSEN
EDUCATIONAL SERVICES

CAM

Published in 2017 by Britannica Educational Publishing (a trademark of Encyclopædia Britannica, Inc.) in association with The Rosen Publishing Group, Inc.
29 East 21st Street, New York, NY 10010

Distributed exclusively by Rosen Publishing.
To see additional Britannica Educational Publishing titles, go to rosenpublishing.com.

First Edition

Britannica Educational Publishing
J.E. Luebering: Executive Director, Core Editorial
Anthony L. Green: Editor, Compton's by Britannica

Rosen Publishing
Kathy Kuhtz Campbell: Senior Editor
Nelson Sá: Art Director
Michael Moy: Designer
Cindy Reiman: Photography Manager
Nicole Baker: Photo Researcher
Supplementary material by Trenton Campbell

Library of Congress Cataloging-in-Publication Data

Names: Campbell, Trenton, editor.
Title: Drawing : materials, techniques, styles, and practice / Edited by Trenton Campbell.
Description: New York : Britannica Educational Publishing in Association with
  Rosen Educational Services, 2017. | Series: Britannica's Practical Guide to the Arts | Includes bibliographical references and index.
Identifiers: LCCN 2015047448 | ISBN 9781680483710 (library bound : alk. paper)
Subjects: LCSH: Drawing--Technique--Juvenile literature. | Artists' materials--Juvenile literature.
Classification: LCC NC730 .D75 2016 | DDC 741.2--dc23
LC record available at http://lccn.loc.gov/2015047448

Manufactured in China

INTRODUCTION vi

CHAPTER ONE
**THE ELEMENTS AND PRINCIPLES
OF DESIGN IN DRAWING** 1
    A SKETCH 6
PLANE TECHNIQUES 8
    PERSPECTIVE 9
THE DRAWING SURFACE 12
**THE RELATIONSHIP BETWEEN DRAWING
AND OTHER ART FORMS** .13
SURFACES 15

CHAPTER TWO
**TOOLS AND TECHNIQUES AND THE
PRESERVATION OF WORKS ON PAPER** 18
CHARCOAL 20
    KÄTHE KOLLWITZ 22
CHALKS 24
METALPOINTS 30
    ALBRECHT DÜRER 32
GRAPHITE POINT 39
    PENCIL DRAWING 40
COLOURED CRAYONS 44
    PASTEL 44
INCISED DRAWING 46
BRUSH, PEN, AND DYESTUFFS 47
  PENS 47
    QUILL, REED, AND METAL PENS 50
  INKS 49
    BISTRE AND SEPIA 54

PEN DRAWINGS. 56
  THE PICASSO MUSEUM 60
  BRUSH DRAWINGS. 61
WASH DRAWING 62
COMBINATIONS OF VARIOUS
TECHNIQUES. 65
  CLAUDE LORRAIN .66
MECHANICAL DEVICES 73
  CAMERA OBSCURA 74
THE CONSERVATION AND RESTORATION OF
PRINTS AND DRAWINGS ON PAPER. 77

CHAPTER THREE
APPLIED DRAWINGS 81
TECHNICAL DRAWINGS .81
ARCHITECTURAL DRAWINGS. 81
  A PANTOGRAPH. 82
  LOUIS SULLIVAN 86
TOPOGRAPHIC AND CARTOGRAPHIC
DRAWINGS 89
SCIENTIFIC ILLUSTRATIONS 89
  JOHN JAMES AUDUBON. 90
ILLUSTRATIVE DRAWINGS 93
ILLUSTRATIONS 93
  SCRATCHBOARD .94
CARICATURE. 95
CARTOONS 95
  AL HIRSCHFELD. .96

CHAPTER FOUR
SUBJECT MATTER 99

PORTRAITS 100
    HANS HOLBEIN THE YOUNGER 103
LANDSCAPES 110
    THE DANUBE SCHOOL 112
FIGURE COMPOSITIONS AND STILL LIFES 114
    ODILON REDON 116
FANCIFUL AND NONREPRESENTATIONAL
DRAWINGS 117
    WALTER CRANE 118
ARTISTIC ARCHITECTURAL DRAWINGS 121
    GIOVANNI BATTISTA PIRANESI 122

CHAPTER FIVE
THE HISTORY OF DRAWING 124
WESTERN HISTORY 124
  THE 14TH, 15TH, AND 16TH CENTURIES 125
    JACOPO BELLINI .127
    LEONARDO DA VINCI'S NOTEBOOKS AND
    ANATOMICAL STUDIES 130
  THE 17TH, 18TH, AND 19TH CENTURIES 140
    JACQUES CALLOT 141
    THOMAS ROWLANDSON 146
EASTERN HISTORY 148
    HOKUSAI 150

CONCLUSION 157
GLOSSARY 162
BIBLIOGRAPHY 165
INDEX 176

D rawing is the art or technique of producing images on a surface, usually paper, by means of marks, usually of ink, graphite, chalk, charcoal, or crayon. Drawing is a kind of universal language. The scribbles of children are drawings as truly as are the sketches of the masters. Children make marks on surfaces long before they learn to write. It is easy to understand, therefore, that drawing is the most fundamental of the arts and is closely related to all the others. Writing itself is simply the drawing of letters, which are symbols for sounds.

Although drawings differ in quality, they have a common purpose—to give visible form to an idea and to express the artist's feeling about it. As an art form, drawing is the translation of the idea and the emotion into a form that can be seen and felt by others.

The same can be said of painting. Indeed, most paintings first take form as drawings, although different methods and materials are used to complete them. Drawing is generally less laborious than painting, which means that it can be more spontaneous. The preliminary drawing may reveal more of the artist's feeling about the subject than the polished final work. In a great drawing is displayed not only technical skill, but also the artist's intense emotion at the moment of creation.

Personal feeling is clearly seen in the work of Giovanni Battista Tiepolo, a Venetian who lived in the 18th century. His drawing is full of the sunny brightness found in the work of the Venetians. In striking contrast is the drawing

Michelangelo drew *Profile with Oriental Headdress*, a sanguine drawing on coloured paper, c. 1522. A sanguine is a chalk or crayon drawing done in a blood-red, reddish, or flesh-tone colour.

of Fernand Léger, a French artist of the 20th century. Léger composed drawings with mechanical precision. As a follower of the Cubist school, he reduced natural forms to geometrical shapes. His style permitted him to break down objects and reassemble them in his own way to get the effect he wanted.

In addition to the way in which they feel about their subjects, artists reflect in their drawing their individual approaches to techniques and tools. Pure line is the simplest technical approach to drawing. In line drawings, form is usually expressed by line only. There is no attempt to distinguish between light and dark. Master drafters have discovered that understatement, or the skillful use of a few lines, will usually result in a better drawing. Relative distance forward and backward is frequently achieved by emphasizing the width or depth of certain lines, particularly those closest to the observer.

Line drawing was used in Asian, Egyptian, and early Greek art. Its influence can be traced through Byzantine and medieval work, particularly where the Asian influence was strong. Such a drawing is the 16th-century Persian pen sketch *Camel with Driver*. In this composition the animal and driver are drawn in rounded outline. Only a few evidences of textural treatment are found on the camel's head, tail, and forelegs.

To show form and shadow, an artist may draw a set of closely spaced lines called hatching, or two sets of intersecting lines called crosshatch lines. These devices, together with sharply accented highlights, were used by such masters as Rembrandt.

Most artists have used combinations of line and form techniques. The drawings of Michelangelo, however, represent pure form drawings. He makes the viewer feel the roundness of his figures.

Perspective and foreshortening have been used by some artists to give depth to their drawings. Objects in the distance usually are made smaller, and the receding edges of forms seem to converge at one or more vanishing points. Other artists abstract the essential features of a form without in any way representing the form in an imitative style. Still other artists use drawing to produce emotional effects. Short, jagged lines might indicate intense anger; broad curves might signify contentment.

The character of a drawing is also conditioned by the tools that the artist uses in its development and by the material on which the artist draws. Most drawings are done on paper, which may vary in weight, surface texture, and colour.

Smooth papers are most likely to be used for fine pen and pencil drawings. Rough surfaces are most preferred for dry brush drawings. Coloured papers may be used when the artist wants to give tonal background to a chalk or charcoal sketch.

Pen and ink have been used by artists since ancient times. During the Middle Ages pens were made from goose quills. Nowadays, drawing pens are available with metal nibs of varying width. Black India ink and other kinds and colours are used today. The Chinese liked to use brush and ink, and this combination is still common.

Pencils did not come into general use until after 1800. Now many different sizes and shapes are available, with a wide range of hard and soft leads. Softer leads make blacker impressions. Chalk and charcoal have been used for drawing since ancient times. They are limited in use because they smear easily, but such artists as Michelangelo and Edgar Degas developed tonal effects by rubbing them into the surface of the paper. Crayons have the advantage of colour. Pastel colours are made of finely ground crayon pigment with a small quantity of gum or resin to hold the particles together. Pastel allows soft effects in a full range of colours.

Works that are produced with the tools of graphic arts are similar to drawings but can exist in many copies. The graphic artist may do the original "drawing" on stone (for a lithograph), on a metal plate (for an engraving or etching), or on wood (for a woodcut).

Drawing as formal artistic creation might be defined as the primarily linear rendition of objects in the visible world, as well as of concepts, thoughts, attitudes, emotions, and fantasies given visual form, of symbols and even of abstract forms. This definition, however, applies to all graphic arts and techniques that are characterized by an emphasis on form or shape rather than mass and colour, as in painting. Drawing as such differs from graphic printing processes in that a direct relationship exists between production and result. Drawing, in short, is the end product of a successive effort applied directly to the carrier. Whereas a drawing may form the basis for reproduction or copying, it is nonetheless unique by its very nature.

Although not every artwork has been preceded by a drawing in the form of a preliminary sketch, drawing is in effect the basis of all visual arts. Often the drawing is absorbed by the completed work or destroyed in the course of completion. Thus, the usefulness of a ground plan drawing of a building that is to be erected decreases as the building goes up. Similarly, points and lines marked on a raw stone block represent auxiliary drawings for the sculpture that will be hewn out of the material. Essentially, every painting is built up of lines and pre-sketched in its main contours; only as the work proceeds is it consolidated into coloured surfaces. As shown by an increasing number of findings and investigations, drawings form the material basis of mural, panel, and book paintings. Such preliminary sketches may merely indicate the main contours or may predetermine the final execution down to exact details. They may also be mere probing sketches. Long before the appearance of actual small-scale drawing, this procedure was much used for monumental murals. With sinopia—the preliminary sketch found on a layer of its own on the wall underneath the fresco, or painting on freshly spread, moist plaster—one reaches the point at which a work that merely served as technical preparation becomes a formal drawing expressing an artistic intention.

Not until the late 14th century, however, did drawing come into its own—no longer necessarily subordinate, conceptually or materially, to another art form. Autonomous, or independent, drawings, as the name implies, are themselves the ultimate aim of an artistic effort; therefore, they are usually characterized by a pictorial structure and by precise execution down to details.

Formally, drawing offers the widest possible scope for the expression of artistic intentions. Bodies, space, depth, substantiality, and even motion can be made visible through drawing. Furthermore, because of the immediacy of its statement, drawing expresses the draftsman's personality spontaneously in the flow of the line; it is, in fact, the most personal of all artistic statements. It is thus plausible that the esteem in which drawing was held should have developed parallel to the value placed on individual artistic talent. Ever since the Renaissance, drawing has gradually been losing its anonymous and utilitarian status in the eyes of artists and the public, and its documents have been increasingly valued and collected.

Drawing has been the backbone of commercial art. Industries that use drawings include advertising, fashion, and publishing—especially children's books. No edition of Lewis Carroll's *Alice's Adventures in Wonderland*, for example, would be complete without Sir John Tenniel's illustrations. Commercial artists also illustrate textbooks and reference books.

Drawings in comic strips, comic books, and graphic novels are called cartoons. Many drawings, each varying only slightly from the last, make up a scene in a traditional animated cartoon. A caricature is a cartoon that exaggerates a situation or a person's characteristics, usually for purposes of ridicule or satire. Political cartoons are caricatures that appear in daily newspapers. The angry cartoons of Thomas Nast are credited with helping to bring down the Tweed Ring, a political machine that controlled New York City in the 19th century.

Drawing: Materials, Technique, Styles, and Practice deals with the aesthetic characteristics, the mediums of expression, the subject matter, some leading artists and their works, and the history of drawing.

THE ELEMENTS AND PRINCIPLES OF DESIGN IN DRAWING

The principal element of drawing is the line. Through practically the entire development of Western drawing, though essentially abstract, not present in nature, and appearing only as a border setting of bodies, colours, or planes, the line has been the vehicle of a representational more or less illusionist rendition of objects. Only in very recent times has the line been conceived of as an autonomous element of form, independent of an object to be represented.

Conscious and purposeful drawing represents a considerable mental achievement: the ability to reduce three-dimensional objects in space

Jean-Auguste-Dominique Ingres drew violinist Niccolò Paganini, c. 1819, with delicate yet firm lines.

to lines drawn on a single plane. That ability presupposes a great gift for abstraction. The identification of the motif of a drawing by the viewer is no less an achievement, although it is mastered by practically all human beings. The visual interpretation of a line as a representation of a given object is made possible through certain forms of that line that call forth associations. The angular meeting of two lines, for example, may be considered as representing the borders of a plane; the addition of a third line can suggest the idea of a cubic body. Vaulting lines stand for arches, convergent lines for depth.

With the aid of this modest basic vocabulary, one can distill comprehensible images from a variety of linear phenomena. The simple outline sketch—Greek legend has it that the first "picture" originated from copying the shadows on the sand—represents one of the oldest and most popular possibilities of graphic rendition. After decisively characterizing the form of Egyptian drawing and the archaic art of Greece, the outline sketch became the chief vehicle of artistic communication in late antiquity and the Middle Ages. Used in a variety of ways in the early Renaissance, it became dominant once again in Neoclassicism, as it is, for that matter, in the classicist period of a given artist's total work.

The outline sketch is elaborated into the detailed drawing by means of the line, which differentiates between the plastic and the spatial values of the object. Borders of individual objects, changes in the spatial plane, and varying intensities of colour applied within an outline sketch all tend to enrich and clarify the relationship between the whole and its component parts.

The free beginning, the disappearance, or the interruption of a line provides opportunities for gradually slurring an edge until it becomes a plane, for letting colour transitions fade away, for having the line vanish in the depth.

The thickening or thinning of a line can also be used to indicate, spatially or by means of colour, a change in the object designated by that line. Even light-and-shadow values may be rendered by differences in stroke strength.

While the chopping up of a line into several brief segments, and, even more, the drawing of individual lines running parallel in one direction, makes the outlined form appear less corporeal and firm, it reproduces the visual impact of the form in a more pictorial manner. Slight shifts in the flow of the line are intended to represent smooth curves and transitions; they also reinforce the effect of light striking a surface and thus give the corporeal appearance. Finally, short, curving segments of a line that do not stand in a clearly angular relationship to one another but are arranged on the sheet in loose formation allow the pictorial and colour component to dominate, as in the work of the 16th-century Italian artist Jacopo Tintoretto. An extreme case is the complete dissolution of the linear stroke into dots and spots, as, for example, in the drawings of the 19th-century Pointillist painter Georges Seurat.

A mere combination of these varied shapes of the line, without reference to the mediums in which the lines are drawn, provides the artist with a plethora of subjective opportunities for the expression both of general stylistic traits and of personal characteristics.

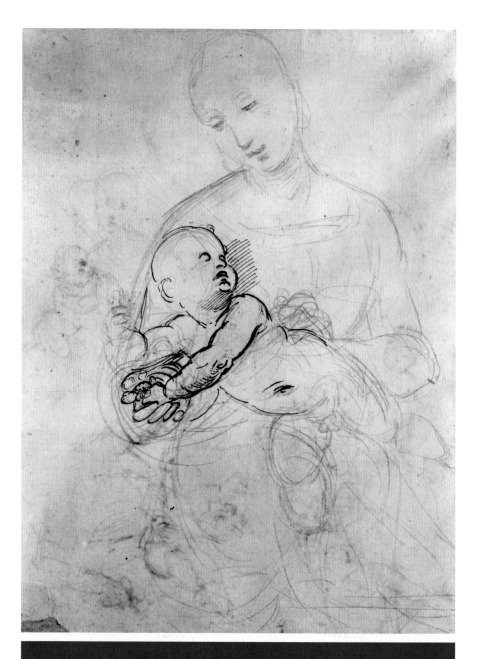

Raphael used black chalk and pen to sketch *Madonna and Child* (c. 1506), a drawing that shows the artist's use of soft lines.

An arrangement of forceful, mainly straight strokes in accentuated, sharp angles lends the drawing an austere character emphasizing dramatic and expressive traits. This method of drawing, in fact, is characteristic of stylistic epochs and artistic regions (not to mention individual artists) that prefer these qualities: during the Renaissance in the rather sober city of Florence, in early-20th-century German Expressionist works, where it is used to convey mood, but also in the drawings of Rembrandt (17th century) and Vincent van Gogh (late 19th century). Soft lines, on the other hand, running in drawn-out, smoothly rounded forms and stressing graphic regularity above any statement of content, constitute the formal equivalent to elegant, courtly, and lyric qualities of expression. Accordingly, they are often found in drawings of the Soft style; in the early Renaissance, particularly in the work of artists from the Italian province of Umbria and in young Raphael's sketches; in the work of Nazarenes, a 19th-century group of Romantic painters whose subjects were mainly religious; in the Jugendstil, a late-19th- and early-20th-century German decorative style parallel to Art Nouveau in its organic foliate forms, sinuous lines, and non-geometric curves; and in a very pure form in one of the classic draftsmen, the 19th-century French painter Jean-Auguste-Dominique Ingres. A markedly even-stroke texture, with waxing and waning lines in regular proportions and evenly distributed within the page, brings drawing close to calligraphic writing and is found in all stylistic epochs that value ornamentation.

The technique of hatching gives the line an additional potential for the clarification of plastic

A SKETCH

Traditionally, a sketch is a rough drawing or painting in which an artist notes down his preliminary ideas for a work that will eventually be realized with greater precision and detail. The term also applies to brief creative pieces that per se may have artistic merit.

In a traditional sketch, the emphasis usually is laid on the general design and composition of the work and on overall feeling. Such a sketch is often intended for the artist's own guidance; but sometimes, in the context of a bottega (studio-shop) type of production, in which an artist would employ many assistants, sketches were made by the master for works to be completed by others. There are three main types of functional sketches. The first–sometimes known as a croquis–is intended to remind the artist of some scene or event he has seen and wishes to record in a more permanent form. The second– a pochade–is one in which he records, usually in colour, the atmospheric effects and general impressions of a landscape. The third type is related to portraiture and notes the look on a face, the turn of a head, or other physical characteristics of a prospective sitter.

From the 18th century, however, sketch came to take on a new meaning, which has almost come to supersede the traditional one. The emphasis on freshness and spontaneity, which was an integral part of the Romantic attitude, the fact that there was a great increase in the number of amateur artists, and the growing appreciation of nature, accompanied by an expansion of facilities for travel, transformed the sketch into something regarded as an end in itself–a slight and unpretentious picture, in some simple medium (pen and ink, pencil, wash, or watercolour) recording a visual experience. This led to a revaluation of sketches that had originally been created for other works. Contemporary taste, for instance, tends to value John Constable's sketches as highly as his finished works.

relationships and of light phenomena. In hatching, parallel, short, equidistant, more or less straight lines create static and tectonic (structural) values by marking individual body planes. Gently curved hatching stresses the roundness of the body and can also accentuate, as tone value, shaded parts of the representation.

Cross-hatching, in which two layers of hatching intersect at right angles, reinforces the body-and-shadow effect. Known since the days of Michelangelo and Albrecht Dürer in the 15th and 16th centuries, this artistic technique is often used with slanted or even curved hachures for the linear rendition of rounded parts. In rigorously monotone drawings, this method is the most suitable for the depiction of spherical bodies.

The human body, with its highly articulated surface, can be modelled in this fashion very clearly and precisely. For 17th- and 18th-century engravers, this process became the most important means of drawing. All of these different possibilities of linear rendition can be achieved with pen and crayon as well as with the brush.

PLANE TECHNIQUES

Linear techniques of drawing are supplemented by plane methods, which can also be carried out with crayon. For example, evenly applied dotting, which is better done with soft mediums, results in an areal effect in uniform tone. Various values of the chiaroscuro (pictorial representation in terms of light and shade without regard to colour) scale can also be rendered by means of dry or moist rubbing. Pulverized drawing materials that are rubbed into the drawing surface result in evenly toned areas that serve both as a closed foundation for linear drawing and as indication of colour values for individual sections.

More significant for plane phenomena, however, is brushwork, which, to be sure, can adopt all linear drawing methods but the particular strength of which lies in stroke width and tone intensity, a medium that allows for extensive differentiation in colour tone and value. Emphases created by the repeated application of the same tone provide illusionistic indentations that can be conceived of spatially and corporeally. Colour differences result from the use of various mediums. Brushwork also lends itself to spatial and plastic representation, just as it can constitute an autonomous value in nonrepresentational drawings.

PERSPECTIVE

Perspective is the method of graphically depicting three-dimensional objects and spatial relationships on a two-dimensional plane or on a plane that is shallower than the original (for example, in flat relief).

Perceptual methods of representing space and volume, which render them as seen at a particular time and from a fixed position and are characteristic of Chinese and most Western painting since the Renaissance, are in contrast to conceptual methods. Pictures drawn by young children and untrained artists, many paintings of cultures such as ancient Egypt and Crete, India, Islam, and pre-Renaissance Europe, as well as the paintings of many modern artists, depict objects and surroundings independently of one another—as they are known to be, rather than as they are seen to be—and from the directions that best present their most characteristic features. Many Egyptian and Cretan paintings and drawings, for example, show the head and legs of a figure in profile, while the eye and torso are shown frontally. This system produces not the illusion of depth but the sense that objects and their surroundings have been compressed within a shallow space behind the picture plane.

(CONTINUED ON THE NEXT PAGE)

(CONTINUED FROM THE PREVIOUS PAGE)

In Western art, illusions of perceptual volume and space are generally created by use of the linear perspectival system, based on the observations that objects appear to the eye to shrink and parallel lines and planes to converge to infinitely distant vanishing points as they recede in space from the viewer. Parallel lines in spatial recession will appear to converge on a single vanishing point, called one-point perspective. Perceptual space and volume may be simulated on the picture plane by variations on this basic principle, differing according to the number and location of the vanishing points. Instead of one-point (or central) perspective, the artist may use, for instance, angular (or oblique) perspective, which employs two vanishing points.

Another kind of system—parallel perspective combined with a viewpoint from above—is traditional in Chinese painting. When buildings rather than natural contours are painted and it is necessary to show the parallel horizontal lines of the construction, parallel lines are drawn parallel instead of converging, as in linear perspective. Often foliage is used to crop these lines before they extend far enough to cause a building to appear warped.

Early European artists used a perspective that was an individual interpretation of what they saw rather than a fixed mechanical method. At the beginning of the Italian Renaissance, early in the 15th century, the mathematical laws

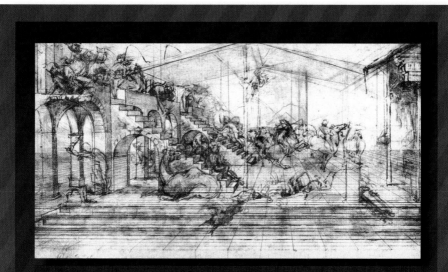

Leonardo created an illusion of depth on a flat surface in this linear perspective study for *The Adoration of the Magi*, c. 1481.

of perspective were discovered by the architect Filippo Brunelleschi, who worked out some of the basic principles, including the concept of the vanishing point, which had been known to the Greeks and Romans but had been lost. These principles were applied in painting by Masaccio (as in his *Trinity* fresco in Santa Maria Novella, Florence, c. 1427), who within a short period brought about an entirely new approach in painting. A style was soon developed using configurations of architectural exteriors and interiors as the background for religious paintings, which thereby acquired the illusion of great spatial depth. In his seminal *Della pittura* (1436; *On Painting*), Leon Battista Alberti codified, especially for painters, much of the practical work on the subject that had been carried out by earlier artists; he formulated, for example, the

(*CONTINUED ON THE NEXT PAGE*)

(*CONTINUED FROM THE PREVIOUS PAGE*)

idea that "vision makes a triangle, and from this it is clear that a very distant quantity seems no larger than a point."

Linear perspective dominated Western painting until the end of the 19th century, when Paul Cézanne flattened the conventional Renaissance picture space. The Cubists and other 20th-century painters abandoned the depiction of three-dimensional space altogether and hence had no need for linear perspective.

Linear perspective plays an important part in presentations of ideas for works by architects, engineers, landscape architects, and industrial designers, furnishing an opportunity to view the finished product before it is begun. Differing in principle from linear perspective and used by both Chinese and European painters, aerial perspective is a method of creating the illusion of depth by a modulation of colour and tone.

All of these effects of monochrome drawing are accentuated with the use of varicoloured mediums of a basic material: for example, coloured chalks, drawing inks, or watercolour. Although these mediums enrich the art of drawing, they do not widen its basic range.

THE DRAWING SURFACE

To these graphic elements must be added another phenomenon the formal significance of which is restricted to drawing: the effect of the unmarked drawing surface, usually paper. Almost all studies (drawings of details), many autonomous sheets, most portrait drawings, as well as figure compositions, still lifes, and even landscapes stand free on the sheet instead of being closed off with a frame-line. Thus, the empty surface, suggesting by itself a spatial background to the drawing on it, contributes actively to the artistic effect.

Even within line composition, the surface left blank fulfills an essential role. Among the details conveyed by the empty space may be the planes of a face, the smooth width of a garment, the mass of a figure or object, the substance the borders and nuances of which are indicated by the drawing. Even the space around individual objects, the spatial distance between them and their environment, the width of a river and the depth of a landscape may be merely signaled by the drawing and filled by the void.

This void can itself become the dominant form enclosed by lines or contours—for example, in decorative sketches and in many ornamental drawings that make use of the negative form, an effect attainable also by tinting the blank planes.

THE RELATIONSHIP BETWEEN DRAWING AND OTHER ART FORMS

The bond between drawing and other art forms is of course very close, because the preliminary sketch was for a long time the chief purpose of the drawing. A state of mutual dependence exists in particular between painting and drawing, above all, in the case of sketches and studies for the composition of a picture. The relationship is closest with preliminary sketches of the same size as the original, the so-called cartoons whose contours were pressed through or perforated for dyeing with charcoal dust. Once transferred to the painting surface, the sketch had served its purpose.

On autonomous sheets, too, the close connection between drawing and painting is evidenced by the stylistic features that are common to both. Drawing and painting agree in many details of content and form. Measurements; proportions of figures; relationship of figure to surrounding space; the distribution of the theme within the composition according to static order, symmetry, and equilibrium of the masses or according to dynamic contrasts, eccentric vanishing points, and over accentuation of individual elements; rhythmic order in separate pictorial units in contrast to continuous flow of lines—all of these formal criteria apply to both art forms. The uniform stylistic character shared by drawing and painting is often less severely expressed in the former because of the spontaneous flow of the unfettered artist's stroke, or "handwriting," and of the struggle for form as recorded in the pentimenti (indications in the drawing that the artist had changed his mind and drawn over his original formulation). Furthermore drawing can stimulate certain aspects of movement more easily than painting can through the rhythmic repetition of a contour or the blended rubbing of a sharp borderline.

Still closer, perhaps, is the bond between drawing and engraving, which works with the same artistic means, with monochrome linearity as its main formal element and with various tone and plane methods closely related to those of drawing.

Drawing is more independent than sculpture because sculpture uses a three-dimensional model. As a result, sculptors' drawings can always claim a greater degree of autonomy.

SURFACES

One can draw on practically anything that has a plane surface (it does not have to be level)—for example, papyrus and parchment, cloth, wood, metals, ceramics, stone, and even walls, glass, and sand. (With some of these, to be sure, another dimension is introduced through indentations that give the visual effect of lines.) Ever since the 15th century, however, paper has been by far the most popular ground.

The technique of paper manufacturing, introduced from East Asia by the Arabs, has remained virtually unchanged for the past 2,000 years. A fibrous pulp of mulberry bark, hemp, bast, and linen rags is drained, pressed, and dried in flat molds. The introduction of wood pulp in the mid-19th century, which enabled manufacturers to satisfy the enormously increased demand for bulk paper, did not affect art paper because paper of

Albrecht Dürer drew *Praying Hands,* c. 1508, on blue-coloured paper that he made himself.

large wood content yellows quickly and is therefore ill-suited for art drawing. The essential preparation of the paper to give it a smooth and even surface for writing or drawing was once done by rubbing it with bone meal, gypsum chalk, or zinc and titanium white in a very thin solution of glue and gum arabic. The proper priming, achieved through repeated rubbing and polishing, was of the utmost importance, especially for metalpoint drawings. If such preparation is too weak, the paper accepts the stroke badly; if it is too strong, the coating cracks and chips under the pressure of the hand. Since the early 15th century, however, the sheets have been given the desired smooth and non-absorbent consistency by dipping them in a glue or alum bath. The addition of glue also made it possible to impart to the pulp paper a quality that permitted pen drawings. Pigments, too, could of course be added to the pulp, and the so-called natural papers—chiefly blue and called Venetian papers after the centre of the retail trade in this commodity—became more and more popular. Whereas the 17th century liked half tints of blue, gray, brown, and green, the 18th preferred warm colours such as ivory and beige, along with blue. Since the 18th century, paper has been manufactured in all conceivable colours and halftones.

The range of quality has also greatly increased since the end of the 18th century to give more painstakingly produced drawing papers. Even in earlier times, the absorbent Japan paper made of mulberry bark enjoyed great popularity. Handmade paper, stronger and free of wood, with an irregular edge, has remained to this day a favourite surface for drawings. Vellum, delicate and without veins, resembles parchment in its smooth surface. Modern watercolour paper is a pure linen paper glued in bulk and absolutely free of fat and alum; its two surfaces are of different grain. For pastel drawings, a firm, slightly rough surface is indicated, whereas pen drawings are best done on a very smooth paper.

Granulated and softer drawing tools, such as charcoal, chalk, and graphite are not as dependent on a particular type of paper; but, because of their slight adhesiveness, they often require a stronger bond with the foundation as well as some form of surface protection. This process of fixing was formerly done through repeated varnishing with gum-arabic solution and even with glue or egg-white emulsion. Modern siccatives (drying substances) inhibit discoloration but cannot prevent the living surface from appearing sealed, as it were, under a skin. In pastels especially, the manifold prismatic effects of finely powdered coloured crayons are thus lost, and the bright and airy surface is turned into an amorphous, heavy layer. Pastels, which brush off easily, are therefore best preserved under glass.

TOOLS AND TECHNIQUES AND THE PRESERVATION OF WORKS ON PAPER

Such varied tools as slate pencils, charcoal, metal styli, and chalks may be used for drawing as well as all writing utensils, including pens, pencils, and brushes. Indeed, even chisels and diamonds are used for drawing, not to mention saws, drills, and fire. Dry drawing tools differ in effectiveness from liquid ones because it is not irrelevant from the artistic point of view whether one uses a self-drawing medium that permits an evenly flowing line dependent only on hand pressure or a transferring tool that must be put down periodically and refilled, with resultant differences in the strength and concentration of the line. Modern drawing mediums that combine both possibilities, such as fountain pens, ball-point pens, and fibre-tipped (felt-tipped) pens, are recent inventions.

No less varied than the nature and composition of these drawing mediums is their aesthetic effect. It would nevertheless be wrong to systematize the art of drawing on the basis of the techniques applied; not only does almost every technique have several applications but it can also be combined with other techniques, and the draftsman's temperament inevitably plays a role as

Some common artist's drawing tools are graphite pencils, charcoal sticks, grease pencils (china markers), and crayons.

well. Even if certain techniques predominate in certain periods, the selection of drawing mediums depends on the intended effect and not vice versa. Artists have always been able to attain the desired effect with a variety of techniques. Dry mediums, for example, are predestined for clear lines, liquid ones for plane application. Yet extremely fine strokes can also be made by brush, and broad fields can be marked in with pencil or crayon. Some mediums, including charcoal, one of the oldest, if not the oldest of all, allow both extremes.

CHARCOAL

In every hearth or fireplace, partially consumed pieces of wood remain that can be used as a convenient tool for drawing. Evidence of charcoal sketches for mural, panel, and even miniature paintings can still occasionally be seen under the pigment. Drawing charcoal produced from wood that is as homogeneous as possible gives a porous and not very adhesive stroke. The pointed charcoal pencil permits hair-thin lines; if used broadside on the surface, it creates evenly toned planes. Rubbing and pulverizing the charcoal line results in dimmed intermediate shades and delicate transitions. Because of its slight adhesiveness, charcoal is eminently suited to corrective sketching; but if the drawing is to be preserved, it must be protected by a fixative.

As a medium for quick, probing sketches and practice in studying models, charcoal was once much used in all academies and workshops. The rapid notation of difficult poses, such as Tintoretto demanded of his models, could be done quickly and easily with the adaptable charcoal pencil. While some of these sheets were deemed worthy of preservation, hundreds have surely been lost.

Charcoal has often been used for portrait drawings to preserve for the eventual painting pictorial tints that were already present in the preliminary sketch. When destined to be autonomous portraits, charcoal drawings are executed in detail; with their sharp accents and delicate modeling, such portraits cover the whole range of the medium. In *Portrait of a Lady* (c. 1879), by the 19th-century French painter Édouard Manet, the grain of the wood in the chair, the fur trimming on the dress, the compactness of the coiffure, and the softness of the flesh are all rendered in the same material: charcoal. Popular as that material was for studies and sketches, it has been used for independent drawings destined for preservation by only a few artists; for example, the 17th-century Dutch painter Paulus Potter. It is somewhat more frequent among the great draftsmen of the 19th and 20th centuries, such as Edgar Degas, Henri de Toulouse-Lautrec, Käthe Kollwitz, and Ernst Barlach.

Oiled charcoal, with the charcoal pencils dipped in linseed oil, provides better adhesion and a deeper black. Used in the 16th century by Tintoretto, this technique was applied above all by the Dutch draftsmen of the 17th century in order to set deep-black accents. The advantage of better adhesion in the indentations of the paper in contrast to dry charcoal, which sticks to the elevations, has to be paid for, however, by "incorrigibility"; i.e., correction cannot be made. In addition, charcoal crayons that have been deeply dipped in oil show a brownish streak left by the oil alongside the lines; this technique was used in the 20th century by the American artist Susan Rothenberg.

KÄTHE KOLLWITZ

Käthe Kollwitz (1867–1945) was a German graphic artist and sculptor who was an eloquent advocate for victims of social injustice, war, and inhumanity.

The artist grew up in a liberal middle-class family and studied painting in Berlin (1884–85) and Munich (1888–89). Impressed by the prints of fellow artist Max Klinger, she devoted herself primarily to graphic art after 1890, producing etchings, lithographs, woodcuts, and drawings. In 1891 she married Karl Kollwitz, a doctor who opened a clinic in a working-class section of Berlin. There she gained firsthand insight into the miserable conditions of the urban poor.

Kollwitz's first important works were two separate series of prints, respectively entitled *Weavers' Revolt* (c. 1894–98) and *Peasants' War* (1902–08). In those works she portrayed the plight of the poor and oppressed with the powerfully simplified, boldly accentuated forms that became her trademark. The death of her youngest son in battle in 1914 profoundly affected her, and she expressed her grief in another cycle of prints that treat the themes of a mother protecting her children and of a mother with a dead child. From 1924 to 1932 Kollwitz also worked on a granite monument for her son, which

Käthe Kollwitz prepared an exhibition of her prints and drawings in 1927 in the Academy of Arts in Berlin, Germany.

depicted her husband and herself as grieving parents. In 1932 it was erected as a memorial in a cemetery near Ypres, Belgium.

Kollwitz greeted the Russian Revolution of 1917 and the German revolution of 1918 with hope, but she eventually became disillusioned with Soviet communism. During the years of the Weimar Republic, she became the first woman to be elected a member of the Prussian Academy of Arts, where from 1928 to 1933 she was head of the Master Studio for Graphic Arts. Kollwitz continued to devote herself to socially effective, easily understood art. The Nazis' rise to power in Germany in 1933 led to her forced

(CONTINUED ON THE NEXT PAGE)

(CONTINUED FROM THE PREVIOUS PAGE)

resignation from the academy.

Kollwitz's last great series of lithographs, *Death* (1934–36), treats that tragic theme with stark and monumental forms that convey a sense of drama. In 1940 her husband died, and in 1942 her grandson was killed in action during World War II. The bombing of Kollwitz's home and studio in 1943 destroyed much of her life's work. She died a few weeks before the end of the war in Europe.

Kollwitz was the last great practitioner of German Expressionism and is often considered to be the foremost artist of social protest in the 20th century. A museum dedicated to Kollwitz's work opened in Cologne, Germany, in 1985, and a second museum opened in Berlin one year later. *The Diary and Letters of Kaethe Kollwitz* was published in 1988.

CHALKS

The chalks, which resemble charcoal pencils in outward appearance, are an equally important drawing medium. If charcoal was primarily a medium for quick sketching that could be corrected and for the search for artistic form, chalk drawing, which can also fulfill all of these functions, has steadily gained in importance as an autonomous vehicle of expression. Since the end of the 15th century, stone chalk, as found in nature, has become increasingly more significant in art drawing. As a basic material, alumina chalk has various degrees of hardness, so that the stroke varies from slightly granular to homogeneously dense and smooth.

The attempt to produce a crayon or pencil of the greatest possible uniformity has led to the production of special chalks for drawing; that is, chalks, which, after being pulverized, washed, and molded into convenient sticks, allow a softer and more regular stroke and are also free of sandy particles. The admixture of pigments (carbons in the case of black chalks) creates various tints from a rich black to a brownish gray; compared to the much-used black chalk, the brown variety is of little significance. White chalk, also found in nature, is rarely employed as an independent medium for drawing, although it is frequently used in combination with other mediums to achieve reflections of light as individual accents of plastic modeling.

Beginning with the 15th century, chalk has been used increasingly for studies and sketches. Its suitability for drawing exact lines of any given width and also for laying on finely shaded tints makes it particularly appropriate for modeling studies. Accents that stress plastic phenomena are applied by varying the pressure of the hand. Characteristic details in portrait drawings in particular can be brought out in this manner. Pictorial values as well as light and shadow effects can be rendered with chalk without losing their firm, plastic form. For the same reason, chalk is also most valuable in sketching out paintings and indicating their values.

All of these qualities explain why chalk is such a good medium for autonomous drawings. Indeed, there is scarcely a draftsman who has not worked in chalk, often in combination with other mediums. Aside from portrait drawings done all over the world, landscapes have formed the main theme of chalk drawings, especially with the Dutch, in whose art landscape drawings have played a large role. Ever since the invention of artificial chalk made of lampblack (a fine, bulky, dull-black soot deposited in incomplete combustion of carbonaceous materials), which possesses a precisely measurable consistency—an invention ascribed to Leonardo da Vinci—the pictorial qualities of chalk drawing have been fully utilized. Chalks range from those that are dry and charcoal-like to the fatty ones used by lithographers.

Another very important drawing pencil is similarly a chalk product: the red pencil, or sanguine, contains ferric oxide, which occurs in nature in shadings from dark brown to strong red, and can also be manufactured from the same aluminum-oxide base with ferric oxide or rust added. Besides the stronger pictorial effect possible because of its chromatic value, sanguine also possesses a greater suppleness and solubility in water. Thus, a homogeneous plane can be created through moist rubbing, a compact stroke through liquid linear application, a very delicate tone through light wiping. Although this oxide was used for red tints in prehistoric painting, sanguine does not seem to have acquired artistic dignity until the 15th century, when it became customary to fix drawings by painting them over with a gum solution, for sanguine has no more adhesiveness than charcoal. In the 15th century, sanguine was a popular drawing medium because of its wealth of pictorial possibilities. Those inclined to be

colourists—such as the portraitists Jean Clouet and
Hans Holbein, the Flemish painters around Peter Paul
Rubens, and, above all, the French artists of the 18th
century—particularly favoured it. The possibilities of
sanguine range from suggestive forms with markedly
plastic values to a very pictorial, soft rendition of visual
surface stimuli.

A combination of various chalks offers still richer
colouristic possibilities. Black chalk and sanguine have
been widely used since the 16th century to achieve
colour differentiation between flesh tones, hair, and
the material of garments. The combination of black
and white chalk serves plastic modeling, as does that
of the softer sanguine with white chalk; in the former
case, the accentuation rests with the black, in the latter, with the more suggestive delineation in white.

A decidedly colouristic method lies in the combination of various chalk colours with one another and
with tinted paper. Such pictorially executed sheets,
called à deux crayons (with two colours) and à trois
crayons (with three colours), respectively, were especially popular in 17th- and 18th-century France.
Antoine Watteau reached a previously unheard of
harmony of different chalks on natural paper. With the
three colours, Nicolas Lancret, Jean-Étienne Liotard,
Jacques-André Portail, François Boucher—to name
but a few such artists—achieved sensitive drawings
that are very appealing colouristically.

An additional colour refinement is made possible
with pastel crayons. An ample selection of dry colour
pigments in pastel crayons, prepared with a minimum
of agglutinants and compounded with different shades
of white for the articulation of tints, is commercially

Odilon Redon's unique use of powdery and pungent hues in pastels can be seen in this example, *Bouquet in a Blue Vase* (c. 1905), in which he also used pencil on coloured paper.

available. The colours can be laid on in linear technique directly with the crayons, but an area application made with a piece of soft suede or directly, with the fingers, is more frequent. Although this technique was known to the Accademia degli Incamminati (to the painter Guido Reni, for example) as early as the 17th century, it did not reach its flowering until the 18th century, especially in France (with Jean-Marc Nattier and Jean-Baptiste-Siméon Chardin) and in Venice (with Rosalba Carriera). Pastel chalks are particularly favoured for portraits; their effect approximates that of colour-and-area painting rather than line drawing.

In the 19th and 20th centuries, Degas reverted to a stronger accentuation of the delineatory aspects of drawing. With intermediate varnishes he achieved an overlay drawing with different colours and thus an increased emphasis on individual strokes. This technique, fundamentally different from the older one, was imitated with minor variations by Odilon Redon, Gustave Moreau, Jean-Édouard Vuillard, Pierre Bonnard, and others. It has also been borrowed by such Expressionist artists as Edvard Munch and Ernst Ludwig Kirchner.

Modern grease chalks offer a chromatic scale of similar range. Developed originally for such technical purposes as the lettering of very smooth surfaces, such as metal or glass, they can be applied in the same flat manner as pastels, although with the opposite aesthetic effect: that of compact colours. It was the 20th-century English sculptor Henry Moore who first and convincingly exploited the feasibility of continuing, with other mediums, such as pen or watercolour, work on the firm surface that had been led out with grease chalks.

METALPOINTS

Metalpoints have been used for writing and delineation ever since the scriptoria of antiquity. It required little imagination to employ them also in drawing. The most frequently used material was soft lead, which on a smooth surface comes out pale gray, not very strong in colour, and easily erasable but very suitable for preliminary sketches. Aside from lead, tin and copper were also used, as well as sundry lead-and-pewter alloys. The 15th-century Venetian painter Jacopo Bellini's book of sketches in London

Jacopo Bellini drew *The Nativity*, c. 1450, in leadpoint. This drawing on parchment is from one of his sketchbooks now at the Louvre in Paris.

with leadpoint drawings on tinted paper is a particularly valuable example of this technique, even if individual portions and, indeed, entire pages that had become effected were drawn over long ago. One can see little more than the traces left by the pencil because, as in many other metalpoint drawings, the sketches were redrawn in another medium. Botticelli, for example, sketched with a leadpoint the outline of his illustrations to Dante's *Divine Comedy*, retracing them afterward with the pen. Metalpoints were used into the 18th century for perspectivist constructions and auxiliary delineation, especially in architectural drawings.

More suited to permanent drawing is the silverpoint, which requires special preparation of the foundation and, once applied, cannot be corrected. Its stroke, also pale gray, oxidizes into brown and adheres unerasably. Silverpoint drawings accordingly require a clearer concept of form and a steady hand because corrections remain visible. Because too much pressure can bring about cracks in the foundation, the strokes must be even; emphases, modeling, and light phenomena must be rendered either by means of dense hachures, repetitions, and blanks or else supplemented by other mediums. Despite these difficulties, silverpoint was much used in the 15th and 16th centuries. Dürer's notebook on a journey to Holland shows landscapes, portraits, and various objects that interested him drawn in this demanding technique. Silverpoint was much in demand for portrait drawings from the 15th into the 17th century; revived in the 18th-century Romantic era, it was also used by modern artists, most notably Picasso.

ALBRECHT DÜRER

Albrecht Dürer (1471–1528) was a Nürnberg painter and printmaker who is generally regarded as the greatest German Renaissance artist.

Dürer began his training as a draftsman in the goldsmith's workshop of his father. His precocious skill is evidenced by a remarkable self-portrait done in 1484, when he was 13 years old, and by *Madonna with Musical Angels,* done in 1485, which is already a finished work of art in the late Gothic style.

In 1486 he was an apprentice to the painter and woodcut illustrator Michael Wohlgemuth. After three years in Wohlgemuth's workshop, he left for a period of travel. In 1490 Dürer completed his earliest known painting, a portrait of his father that heralds the familiar characteristic style of the mature master.

Dürer's years as a journeyman probably took the young artist to the Netherlands, to Alsace, and to Basel, Switzerland, where he completed his first authenticated woodcut, *St. Jerome Curing the Lion*. During 1493 or 1494 Dürer was in Strasbourg for a short time, returning again to Basel to design several book illustrations. An early masterpiece from this period is a self-portrait with a thistle painted on parchment in 1493 .

Albrecht Dürer drew this self-portrait in silverpoint when he was just 13 years old.

(*CONTINUED ON THE NEXT PAGE*)

(*CONTINUED FROM THE PREVIOUS PAGE*)

At the end of May 1494, Dürer returned to Nürnberg, where he soon married Agnes Frey, the daughter of a merchant. In the autumn of 1494 Dürer seems to have undertaken his first journey to Italy, where he remained until the spring of 1495. A number of bold landscape watercolours dealing with subjects from the Alps of the southern Tirol were made on this journey and are among Dürer's most beautiful creations. Depicting segments of landscape scenery cleverly chosen for their compositional values, they are painted with broad strokes, in places roughly sketched in, with an amazing harmonization of detail.

The trip to Italy had a strong effect on Dürer; direct and indirect echoes of Italian art are apparent in most of his drawings, paintings, and graphics of the following decade. While in Venice and perhaps also before he went to Italy, Dürer saw engravings by masters from central Italy. He was most influenced by the Florentine Antonio Pollaiuolo, with his sinuous, energetic line studies of the human body in motion, and by the Venetian Andrea Mantegna, an artist greatly preoccupied with classical themes and with precise linear articulation of the human figure.

The most striking painting illustrating Dürer's growth toward the Renaissance spirit is a self-portrait, painted in 1498. Here Dürer sought to convey, in the representation of his own person, the aristocratic ideal of the Renaissance.

Italian influences were slower to take hold in Dürer's graphics than in his drawings and paintings. Strong late Gothic elements dominate the visionary woodcuts of his *Apocalypse* series (the Revelation of St. John), published in 1498. The woodcuts in this series display emphatic expression, rich emotion, and crowded, frequently overcrowded, compositions. The same tradition influences the earliest woodcuts of Dürer's *Great Passion* series, also from about 1498. Nevertheless, the fact that Dürer was adopting a more modern conception, a conception inspired by classicism and humanism, is indicative of his basically Italian orientation. Many of Dürer's copper engravings are in the same Italian mode. Some examples of them that may be cited are *Fortune* (c. 1496), *The Four Witches (1497), The Sea Monster* (c. 1498), *Adam and Eve* (1504), and *The Large Horse* (1505). Dürer's graphics eventually influenced the art of the Italian Renaissance that had originally inspired his own efforts. His painterly style, however, continued to vacillate between Gothic and Italian Renaissance until about 1500. Then his restless striving finally found definite direction. He seems clearly to be on firm ground in the penetrating half-length portraits of Oswolt Krel, in the portraits of three members of the aristocratic Tucher family of Nürnberg–all dated 1499–and in the *Portrait of a Young Man* of 1500. In 1500 Dürer painted another self-portrait that is a flattering, Christ-like portrayal.

(CONTINUED ON THE NEXT PAGE)

(CONTINUED FROM THE PREVIOUS PAGE)

During this period of consolidation in Dürer's style, the Italian elements of his art were strengthened by his contact with Jacopo de' Barbari, a minor Venetian painter and graphic artist who was seeking a geometric solution to the rendering of human proportions; it is perhaps due to his influence that Dürer began, around 1500, to grapple with the problem of human proportions in true Renaissance fashion.

In the autumn of 1505, Dürer made a second journey to Italy, where he remained until the winter of 1507. Of the Venetian artists, Dürer now most admired Giovanni Bellini, the leading master of Venetian early Renaissance painting, who, in his later works, completed the transition to the High Renaissance.

By February 1507 at the latest, Dürer was back in Nürnberg, where two years later he acquired an impressive house. It is clear that the artistic impressions gained from his Italian trips continued to influence Dürer to employ classical principles in creating largely original compositions. Drawings from this period recall Mantegna and betray Dürer's striving for classical perfection of form through sweeping lines of firmly modeled and simple drapery. Even greater simplicity and grandeur characterize the diptych of *Adam and Eve*, in which the two figures stand calmly in relaxed classical poses against dark, almost bare, backgrounds.

Between 1507 and 1513 Dürer completed a *Passion* series in copperplate engravings, and between 1509 and 1511 he produced the *Small Passion* in woodcuts. Both of these works are characterized by their tendency toward spaciousness and serenity. During 1513 and 1514 Dürer created the greatest of his copperplate engravings: the *Knight, Death and Devil, St. Jerome in His Study,* and *Melencolia I*–all of approximately the same size, about 24.5 by 19.1 cm (9.5 by 7.5 inches). The extensive, complex, and often contradictory literature concerning these three engravings deals largely with their enigmatic, allusive, iconographic details. Finished form and richness of conception and mood merge into a whole of classical perfection. To the same period belongs Dürer's most expressive portrait drawing–one of his mother.

While in Nürnberg in 1512, the Holy Roman emperor Maximilian I enlisted Dürer into his service, and Dürer continued to work mainly for the emperor until 1519. He collaborated with several of the greatest German artists of the day on a set of marginal drawings for the emperor's prayer book.

Dürer had achieved an international reputation as an artist by 1515, when he exchanged works with the illustrious High Renaissance painter Raphael.

In July 1520 Dürer embarked with his wife on a journey through the Netherlands. In Aachen,

(CONTINUED ON THE NEXT PAGE)

(CONTINUED FROM THE PREVIOUS PAGE)

at the October 23 coronation of the emperor Charles V, successor to Maximilian I, Dürer met and presented several etchings to the mystical and dramatic Matthias Grünewald, who stood second only to Dürer in contemporary German art. Dürer returned to Antwerp by way of Nijmegen and Cologne, remaining there until the summer of 1521. He had maintained close relations with the leaders of the Netherlands school of painting. In December 1520 Dürer visited Zeeland and in April 1521 traveled to Bruges and Ghent, where he saw the works of the 15th-century Flemish masters Jan and Hubert van Eyck, Rogier van der Weyden, and Hugo van der Goes, as well as the Michelangelo Madonna. Dürer's sketchbook of the Netherlands journey contains immensely detailed and realistic drawings.

By July the travelers were back in Nürnberg. Dürer devoted his remaining years mostly to theoretical and scientific writings and illustrations, although several well-known character portraits and some important portrait engravings and woodcuts also date from this period.

Dürer died in 1528 and was buried in the churchyard of Johanniskirchhof in Nürnberg. That he was one of his country's most influential artists is manifest in the impressive number of pupils and imitators that he had.

GRAPHITE POINT

Toward the end of the 16th century, a new drawing medium was introduced and soon completely displaced metalpoint in sketching and preliminary drawing: the graphite point. Also called Spanish lead after its chief place of origin, this drawing medium was quickly and widely adopted; but because of its soft and smeary consistency it was used for autonomous drawings only by some Dutch painters, and even they employed it mostly in conjunction with other points. (It might be added that the graphite point was originally taken for a metal because its texture shines metallically in slanting light.) The lead pencil, or more properly *crayon Conté*, became established in art drawing after Nicolas-Jacques Conté invented, around 1790, a manufacturing process similar to that used in the production of artificial chalk. Purified and washed, graphite could henceforth be made with varying admixtures of clay and in any desired degree of hardness. The hard points, with their durable, clear, and thin stroke layers, were especially suited to the purposes of Neoclassicist and Romantic draftsmen. The Germans working in Rome, in particular, took advantage of the chance to sketch rapidly and to reproduce, in one and the same medium, subtle differentiations as well as clear proportions of plasticity and light. Among the most masterful pencil artists of all was Ingres, who pre-sketched systematically in pencil the well-thought-out structure of his paintings.

The more pictorially inclined artists of the late 19th century preferred softer pencils to throw into plastic relief certain areas within the drawing. Seurat, on the other hand, reached back to graphite in his drawings from the concert cafés, among them *At the Concert*

Européen (c. 1886–88), in which he translated the Pointillistic technique (applying dots of colour to a surface so that from a distance they blend together) into the monochrome element of drawing. Pencil frottage (rubbing made on paper laid over a rough surface), first executed by the Surrealist artist Max Ernst, represents a marginal kind of drawing, for here the artist's hand is no longer the sole creator of forms.

PENCIL DRAWING

A pencil drawing is a drawing that is executed with an instrument composed of graphite enclosed in a wood casing and intended either as a sketch for a more elaborate work in another medium, an exercise in visual expression, or a finished work. The cylindrical graphite pencil, because of its usefulness in easily producing linear gray-black strokes, became the successor of the older, metallic drawing stylus, with which late medieval and Renaissance artists and tradesmen sketched or wrote on paper, parchment, or wood.

Although graphite was mined in the 16th century, the use by artists of pieces of natural graphite, inserted in a *porte-crayon* ("pencil holder"), is not known before the 17th century. Then minor graphite details were included in sketches, notably in landscape renderings by Dutch artists. During that century and most of the 18th, graphite was used to make preliminary sketch lines for drawings to be completed in other media, but drawings completely finished with graphite were rare.

Although pencil drawings were much less commonly produced by artists of those centuries than sketches in chalks, charcoal, and pen and ink, the use of graphite gradually increased among painters, miniaturists, architects, and designers. By the late 18th century, an ancestor of the modern pencil was constructed in the form of a rod of natural graphite fitted into a hollow cylinder of wood. Not until 1795, however, did the French inventor Nicolas-Jacques Conté devise a method of producing pencil rods from mixtures of graphite and clays, a true prototype of the modern graphite pencil. Conté's technical improvement made possible the production of fine pencils the strokes of which could be controlled, varying from type to type in softness and hardness, darkness and lightness. These excellent quality graphite pencils encouraged wider use by 19th-century artists, and pencil drawing became commonly used for studies and preliminary sketches. The graphite pencil

(CONTINUED ON THE NEXT PAGE)

(CONTINUED FROM THE PREVIOUS PAGE)

could be used on almost any type of drawing surface, a fact that helped make it indispensable in the artist's studio.

Although graphite pencils provided a substantial range of light–dark effects and the opportunity for tonal modeling, the greatest masters of pencil drawing always kept the elements of a simple linearism or limited shading that were appropriate to pencil drawing. This concept of pencil drawing contrasted with that sometimes employed in the 18th and 19th centuries in which extensive tonal modeling of three-dimensional forms and elaborate effects of light and shade were produced by artists and miniaturists by rubbing the soft graphite particles with a stump, a tightly rolled piece of soft paper or chamois.

The preciseness and clarity associated with the use of a moderately hard graphite pencil were developed in the highly selective draftsmanship of the 19th-century French Neoclassicist Jean-Auguste-Dominique Ingres. His figure sketches and portrait studies were the epitome of pencil drawing in which lucid contours and limited shading combined to create a spirit of elegance and restraint. Many artists throughout Europe accepted this manner, including such German draftsmen as Adrian Ludwig Richter, who preferred the hardest of pencils and sharpest of points to produce wirelike delineations of figures and landscapes. Softer and darker graphite pencils offered appropriate effects to artists whose tastes required more freedom and spontaneity. The sketches of the Romantic artist Eugène Delacroix, created swiftly and filled with flamboyant and undetailed strokes, had a suggestiveness of dramatic figures and compositions. Vincent van Gogh chose a broad carpenter's pencil for powerful, blunt strokes. To emulate the brilliant atmosphere of Provence, Paul Cézanne employed the pencil, especially in his sketchbooks, to produce highly reductive landscape sketches that made expert use of graphite's inherent silvery value.

One of the most sensitive users of the graphite pencil in the 19th century was the French artist Edgar Degas. A master pastelist and draftsman with coloured chalks and charcoal, Degas created pencil drawings of warmth and charm that were quite unlike the cool, classic works of Ingres or the highly animated, sometimes violent sketches of Delacroix. Degas, with high selectivity, combined graciously fluid outlines with soft, limpid tonal shadings.

COLOURED CRAYONS

Coloured crayons, in circulation since the late 19th century, offer all the possibilities of black graphite points; and, in combinations, they attain a stronger colour value than chalks because they do not merge with one another. Every line preserves its original and characteristic colour, a form of independence that Gustav Klimt and Picasso exploited to the full.

PASTEL

Pastel is a dry drawing medium executed with fragile, finger-size sticks. These drawing crayons, called pastels, are made of powdered pigments combined with a minimum of nongreasy binder, usually gum tragacanth or, from the mid-20th century, methyl cellulose. Made in a wide range of colour values, the darkest in each hue consists of pure pigment and binder, the others having varying admixtures of inert whites. Once the colours are applied to paper, they appear fresh and bright. Because they do not change in colour value, the final effect can be seen immediately. Pastel remains on the surface of the paper and thus can be easily obliterated unless protected by glass or a fixative spray of glue size or gum solution. Fixatives, however, have a disadvantage in that they tend to change the tone and flatten the grain of pastel drawings. When pastel is

applied in short strokes or linearly, it is usually classed as drawing; when it is rubbed, smeared, and blended to achieve painterly effects, it is often regarded as a painting medium. The latter technique was principally used until the late 19th century, when the linear method came to be preferred. Special papers for pastel have been made since the 18th century with widely varying textures, some like fine sandpaper, with a flocked or suedelike finish, prominently ribbed or strongly marked by the drying felts.

Pastels originated in northern Italy in the 16th century and were used by Jacopo Bassano and Federico Barocci. The German artist Hans Holbein the Younger and the French artists Jean and François Clouet did pastel portraits in the same period. The greatest popularity of the medium came in the 18th century, when it was primarily used for portraiture. Rosalba Carriera (Italian), Jean-Baptiste Chardin, François Boucher, Maurice-Quentin de La Tour, Jean-Baptiste Perronneau (all French), Jean-Étienne Liotard (Swiss), and Anton Raphael Mengs (German) were among the major masters of pastel. Largely revived and revitalized in the last third of the 19th century by the French artist Edgar Degas, pastels figure importantly in the work of such artists as Auguste Renoir, Henri de Toulouse-Lautrec, Odilon Redon, Gustave Moreau, Édouard Vuillard, Pierre Bonnard (all French), Mary Cassatt (American expatriate), Joan Miró (Spanish), and Paul Klee (Swiss).

INCISED DRAWING

A role apart is that played by incised drawings. Their pronounced linearity gives them the visual appearance of other drawings; materially, however, they represent the opposite principle, that of subtracting from a surface rather than adding to it. Incised drawings are among the oldest documents of human activity. In primitive African cultures, the methods and forms of prehistoric bone and rock drawings have survived into the present. In a decorative and conceivably also symbolic form, incised decorations on pottery have existed for thousands of years; insofar as the comparison is valid, they correspond in every formal respect to applied drawings of the same period. A formal equivalent may also be observed in later times: in the decorative details of implements, especially metal—from the drawings on Greek mirrors, through the jewelry made at the end of the Roman Empire, to the scenes on medieval weapons and, above all, on Renaissance dress armour. More often than not these are drawings that follow certain models rather than free drawings in the sense of sketches.

Logically, one would also have to consider all niello work under the heading of drawing, because the picture in this case is cut out of the metal and filled with a deep black-coloured paste so that it appears to the eye as a linear projection on a plane. In like manner, work with the graver or burin (cutting tools) and with the etching needle on the engraving plate may be considered to parallel in its execution that gradual effort applied directly to the carrier that was defined earlier as the art of drawing. The difference lies in the fact that this work is not a goal in itself but the prerequisite for a printing process that is intended to be repetitive.

BRUSH, PEN, AND DYESTUFFS

Of the many possibilities of transferring liquid dyestuffs onto a plane, two have become particularly significant for art drawing: brush and pen. To be sure, finger painting, as found in prehistoric cave paintings, has occasionally been practiced since the late Renaissance and increasingly so in more recent times. For drawing as such, however, the method is irrelevant. Similarly, the use of pieces of fur, frayed pieces of wood, bundles of straw, and the like is more significant as a first step toward the camel's-hair brush than as indication that these objects were ever drawing mediums in their own right. Although it is antedated by the brush, which in some cultures (East Asia, for example) has remained in continued use, the pen has been the favourite writing and drawing tool ever since classical antiquity.

PENS

The principle of transferring dyestuffs with the pen has remained virtually unchanged for thousands of years. The capillary effect of the split tip, cut at a slant, applies the drawing fluid to the surface (parchment, papyrus, and, since the late Middle Ages, almost exclusively paper) in amounts varying with the saturation of the pen and the pressure exerted by the drawing hand. The oldest form is that of the reed pen; cut from papyrus plants, sedge, or bamboo, it stores a reservoir of fluid in its hollow interior. Its stroke—characteristically powerful, hard, and occasionally forked as a result of stronger pressure being applied to the split tip—became a popular medium of artistic expression only with the

Vincent van Gogh often used reed-pens to create drawings in pen and ink. In this letter to his brother, Theo, in 1888, van Gogh sketched *The Sower*, which was the subject of a painting he was working on.

rise of a subjective view of the artist's personality during the Renaissance. Rembrandt made superb use of the strong, plastic accents of the reed pen, supplementing it as a rule with other pens or brushes. Beginning in the 19th century with the Dutch artist Vincent van Gogh, pure reed-pen drawings with a certain forcefulness of expression have been created by many artists. Expressionists such as George Grosz used the reed pen frequently.

If the selection of the reed pen already implies a formal statement of sorts, that of the quill pen opens up a far wider range of possibilities. Ever since the rise of drawing in Western art—that is, since the late Middle Ages—the quill has been the most frequently used instrument for applying liquid mediums to the drawing surface. The importance accorded to this tool is attested by the detailed instructions in painters' manuals about the fashioning of the pen from wing shafts of geese, swans, and even ravens. The supple tip of the quill, available in varying strengths, permits a relatively wide scale of individual strokes—from soft, thin lines, such as those used in preliminary sketches for illustrations in illuminated books, through waxing and waning lines that allow differentiation within the stroke, to energetic, broad lines. It was only when metal pens began to be made of high-grade steel and in different strengths that they became a drawing implement able to satisfy the demands made by the individual artist's hand.

INKS

Although all dyestuffs of low viscosity lend themselves to pen drawing, the various inks are most often employed. The manufacture of gallnut ink had been

QUILL, REED, AND METAL PENS

Pens are the oldest and most popular of all the drawing media of the Western artist, in part because of the variety of linear effects provided by the three basic types of pens and their adaptability to the changing styles of draftsmanship over many centuries. These three basic types are quill pens, cut from the wing feathers of fowls and birds; reed pens, formed and trimmed from stems of bamboo-like grasses; and metal pens, fabricated from various metals, especially fine steel. The outstanding master of the reed pen, the Dutch artist Rembrandt, used it often in combination with the quill pen and washes to produce the richly suggestive atmospheric illusionism of his works. The reed pen never had the widespread popularity of quill or metal pens, but for special effects it has served artists admirably; Vincent van Gogh, for example, in his last years in the late 1880s used it in his drawings to produce the blunt, powerful strokes that were counterparts of the heavy brush strokes typical of many of his canvases.

Until the acceptance of the modern steel pen, most Western master draftsmen used quill pens. During the Middle Ages the quill pen was used for the fine delineations of images in manuscripts; its nibs, which can be sharpened to extreme fineness, permit the craftsman to create small linear figures or ornamental decorations on the pages or along the borders of the parchment leaves. This characteristic, combined with the flexibility of the quill point, which responds to pressure for varying the widths of lines or forming accents, made it adaptable to the diverse personal styles of draftsmen from the 15th to the end of the 19th century.

The development of excellent steel pens by the Englishman James Perry in the 1830s and the mass production by stamping pens from steel blanks led to the metal pen's supplanting the quill. Nevertheless, artists only reluctantly adopted the steel pen, and most drawings in pen and ink done before the 20th century were still produced with quills. The steel pen is now used for drawing almost exclusively and is available in many shapes, sizes, and degrees of stiffness or flexibility. It has become standard studio equipment of the illustrator, cartoonist, and designer. Pen drawings by such outstanding painters and sculptors as Pablo Picasso, Henri Matisse, and Henry Moore demonstrate the virtue of the steel pen in producing the sharp linear definitions generally preferred by modern masters.

known from the medieval scriptoria (copying rooms set apart for scribes in monasteries). An extract of gallnuts mixed with iron vitriol and thickened with gum-arabic solution produces a writing fluid that comes from the pen black, with a strong hint of purple violet, and dries almost black. In the course of time it turns a darkish brown, so that the writing fluid in old manuscripts and drawings cannot always be identified by the colour alone. In contrast to other brown writing fluids, the more strongly coloured parts of gallnut ink remain markedly darker; and because inks of especially great vitriol content decompose the paper, the drawing, particularly in its more coloured portions, tends to shine through on the reverse side of the sheet. Only industrially produced chemical inks possess the necessary ion balance to forestall this undesirable effect.

Another ink, one that seems to have found no favour as a writing fluid but has nonetheless had a certain popularity in drawing, is bistre, an easily dissolved, light-to-dark-brown transparent pigment obtained from the soot of the lampblack that coats wood-burning chimneys. Its shade depends both on the concentration and on the kind of wood from which it is derived, hardwoods (especially oaks) producing a darker shade than conifers, such as pine. During the pictorially oriented Baroque period, in the 17th and early 18th centuries, the warm tone that can be thinned at will made bistre a popular medium with which to supplement the planes of a pen drawing.

Also derived from a carbon base is India ink, made from the soot of exceptionally hard woods, such as olive or grape vines, or from the fatty lampblack of the oil flame, with gum-arabic mixed in as a binding agent.

This deep-black, thick fluid preserves its dark tone for a long time and can be thinned with water until it becomes a light gray. Pressed into sticks or bars, it was sold under the name of Chinese ink or India ink. This writing fluid, known already in Egypt and used to this day in China and India, has been manufactured in Europe since the 15th century. Favoured in particular by German and Dutch draftsmen because of its strong colour, it lent itself above all to drawing on tinted paper. Since the 19th century, India ink has been the most popular drawing ink for pen drawings, replacing all other dyestuffs in technical sketches. Only very recently have writing inks gained some significance in art drawing—in connection with the practical fountain pen.

Rembrandt drew *Young Woman at Her Toilette*, c. 1635, with a quill pen, India ink with bistre, and ink washes.

For a relatively short time, a dyestuff of animal origin, sepia, obtained from the pigment of the cuttlefish, was used for drawing. Known since Roman times, it did not come into general use until the 18th century. Compared to yellowish bistre, it has a cooler and darker tone, and is brown with a trace of violet. Until the 18th century, it was employed by such amateur painters as the poet Goethe because of its effectiveness in depth; as a primary pigment, however, it has been completely replaced by industrially manufactured watercolours.

Other dyestuffs are of only minor importance compared with these inks, which are primarily used for pen drawings. Minium (red lead) was used in the medieval scriptoria for the decoration of initial letters and also in illustrated pen drawings. Chinese white is easier to apply with a pointed brush because of its thickness; other pigments, among them indigo and green copper sulfate, are rarely found in drawings. For them, too, the brush is a better tool than the pen. The systematically produced watercolours of various shades are almost wholly restricted to technical drawings.

BISTRE AND SEPIA

Bistre is a brown pigment made from boiling the soot of wood. Because bistre is transparent and has no body, it is frequently used in conjunction with pen and ink drawings as a wash, a liquid spread evenly to suggest shadows, and is especially associated with the appearance of the typical "old master drawing."

It was used to its greatest effect in the 17th and 18th centuries, when the bistre wash was especially favoured by such artists as Rembrandt, Claude Lorrain, Alexander Cozens, and Thomas Gainsborough. The pigment is also used by miniaturists.

Sepia, is a dye, coloured brown with a trace of violet, that is obtained from a pigment protectively secreted by cuttlefish or squid. Sepia is obtained from the ink sacs of these invertebrates. The sacs are speedily extracted from the bodies and are dried to prevent putrefaction. The sacs are then dissolved in dilute alkali, and the resulting solution is filtered. The pigment thus obtained is precipitated with dilute hydrochloric acid and is then washed, filtered, and dried. The chemically inert pigment is fairly permanent and is used as a drawing ink and as an artist's watercolour, particularly in monochrome.

As a type of ink, sepia has been known at least since ancient Roman times. Only from Renaissance times onward, however, did sepia become popular as a drawing medium. In the late 18th and 19th centuries it was particularly popular and generally replaced bistre as a medium for making wash drawings. As a primary pigment, it has been superseded in the 20th century by industrially manufactured watercolours.

PEN DRAWINGS

In combination with written texts, pen drawings are among the oldest artistic documents. Already in classical times, texts were illustrated with firm contours and sparse interior details. During the Middle Ages, marginal drawings and book illustrations were time and again pre-sketched, if not definitively executed, with the pen. In book painting, decidedly delineatory styles developed in which the brush was also employed in the manner of a pen drawing: for example, in the Carolingian school of Reims, which produced the Utrecht Psalter in the 9th century, and also in southern Germany, where a separate illustrative form with line drawings was widespread with the *Biblia Pauperum* ("Poor People's Bibles," biblical picture books used to instruct large numbers of people in the Christian faith). The thin-lined outline sketch is also characteristic of the earliest individual drawings of the late Middle Ages and early Renaissance. Sketches after ancient sculptures or after nature as well as compositions dealing with familiar motifs form the main themes of these drawings. Such sheets were primarily used as models for paintings; gathered in sketchbooks, they were often handed on from one generation to the next. The practical usefulness of these drawings is attested by the supplements added to them by younger artists and by the fact that many metalpoint drawings that had become hard to decipher were redrawn with the pen, as shown by the sketchbooks of the 15th-century Italian artist Antonio Pisanello, now broken up and preserved in several different collections.

In the 16th century, the artistic range of the pen drawing reached an individual articulation that it hardly ever attained again. Every artist was free to exploit with the pen the formal possibilities that corresponded to his talents. Thus Leonardo used a precise stroke for his scientific drawings; Raphael produced relaxed sketches, in which he probed for forms and variations of form; Michelangelo drew with short strokes reminiscent of chisel work; Venetian artist Titian contrasted light and dark by means of hachures laid broadly over the completed figures. Among the Northerners, Dürer mastered all the possibilities of pen drawing, from quick notation to the painstakingly executed autonomous drawing, ranging from a purely graphic and delineatory technique to a spatial and plastic modeling one; it is no wonder that he stimulated so many other artists. The subjective attitude of the later 16th century is often expressed more clearly in Mannerist drawings—characterized by spatial incongruity and excessive elongation of the human figures, which are as revelatory of the artist's personality as handwriting—than it is in completed works of painting and sculpture. A special form of exact drawing is found in models for engravings; some of these were directly mounted on the wood block; some anticipate the style of the copperplate engraving in the pen-drawing stage, with waxing and waning lines, delicate stroke layers, and cross-hatching for spatial and plastic effects.

In the 17th century, the pen drawing took second place to combined techniques, especially wash, a sweep or splash of colour, applied with the brush. An open style of drawing that merely hints at contours, along with contrasting thin and powerful strokes, endowed the line itself with expressive qualities. In his numerous drawings, Rembrandt in particular achieved an exceedingly subtle plastic characterization and even light values through the differentiation of stroke layers and the combination of various pens and brushes.

Additional techniques came to the fore in the 18th century, with the pen sketch providing the scaffold for the drawing that was carried out in a pictorial style. Only decorative sketches and practical studies were laid out more often as linear drawings.

The closed, thin-contour drawing regained its importance with Neoclassicism at the end of the 18th century. The Nazarenes (the nickname of the Lucas Brotherhood—later Guild of St. Luke, who lived in monastic style) and Romantics consciously referred to the early Renaissance manner of drawing, modeling with thin lines. With closed contours, carefully set hair-and-shadow strokes, and precise parallel hachures, they attained plastic values by purely graphic means.

This technique was again followed by a more pictorially oriented phase, culminating in the late 19th century in the recognition of drawing as the most immediate and personal expression of the artist's hand. The pure pen drawing took its place by the side of other highly esteemed art forms. The English Art Nouveau artist Aubrey Beardsley at the end of the 19th century applied the direct black–white contrast to planes, while in the 20th century the French master Henri Matisse and the Spanish artist Pablo Picasso reduced the object to a mere line that makes no claim to corporeal illusion. A large number of illustrators, as well as the artists who draw the comic strips, prefer the clear pen stroke. In the Russian artist Wassily Kandinsky's nonrepresentational compositions, finally, the independence of the line as an autonomous formal value became a new theme in drawing. In the hair-thin automatist seismograms (so-called because of their resemblance to the records of earthquakes) of the 20th-century German artist Wols

Pablo Picasso utilized few lines to embody the personality of his friend Igor Stravinsky in this drawing of the composer, c. 1920.

THE PICASSO MUSEUM

A drawing collection that is noted for its size and accessibility for the study and research of one artist's technique is the Picasso Museum, which is also called Musée National Picasso. It is located in Paris and is dedicated to showcasing the paintings, drawings, engravings, and sculptures of the Spanish-born artist Pablo Picasso.

The Picasso Museum opened in Paris in 1985 with a total of 228 paintings, 149 sculptures, and nearly 3,100 drawings and engravings. In addition to the art itself, the museum houses virtually the entire collection of the artist's preliminary studies. In the ensuing years, the museum acquired more items, and by the early 21st century, it had some 5,000 artworks by Picasso.

The collection is housed in the Hôtel Salé, built by the architect Jean de Bouiller between 1656 and 1659 in the Marais district of Paris. The building underwent extensive renovations prior to the museum's opening, and in 2009 it closed for a major expansion. The project was plagued by various troubles, including cost overruns and construction problems, and the museum did not reopen until 2014.

> **The museum exhibits some 400 works, with many of Picasso's larger sculptures gracing the outdoor gardens. Items from his personal collection of works by other artists, including Paul Cézanne, Henri Rousseau, and Henri Matisse, are also displayed.**

(Alfred Otto Wolfgang Schulze), which are sensitive to the slightest stirring of the hand, this theme leads to a new dimension transcending all traditional concepts of a representational art of drawing.

BRUSH DRAWINGS

Although the brush is best suited to the flat application of pigments—in other words, to painting—its use in a clearly delineatory function, with the line dominating and (a crucial property of brush drawing) in monochrome fashion, can be traced back to prehistoric times.

All of the above-mentioned drawing inks have been used as dyes in brush drawings, often with one and the same pigment employed in combined pen-and-brush work. Still greater differentiation in tone is often obtained through concentrated or thinned mediums and with the addition of supplementary ones. To the latter belong chiefly distemper, a paint in which the pigments

WASH DRAWING

A wash drawing is artwork in which a fine layer of colour, usually diluted ink, bistre, or watercolour, is spread with a brush over a broad surface evenly enough so that no brush marks are visible in the finished product. Usually the technique is used in conjunction with lines made by a pen or pencil that define and outline, while the wash provides colour, depth, and volume. The free use of coats of wash first appeared in the works of such 15th-century Italian artists as Sandro Botticelli and Leonardo da Vinci. Within the next 100 years, this technique was so highly developed that two-tone washes were used concurrently, one shading into the other.

Because it was considered especially suitable for landscape, the technique was very popular with the topographical painters of the 18th and 19th centuries, who built up their pictures by superimposing thin washes in the same way that an oil painter would construct a work with successive glazes: a preliminary foundation of monochrome was laid in over the whole surface (except areas left for highlights), and colours were then added, building up toward the final effect.

are mixed with an emulsion of egg or size (animal-skin glue) or both, and watercolours, which can be used along with bistre and drawing ink. Even oils can sometimes be used for individual effects in drawing, as in the works of Jacob Jordaens.

Sinopia, the preliminary sketch for a monumental wall painting, was done with the brush and has all the characteristics of a preparatory, form-probing drawing. The sketch was carried out directly on the appropriate spot and covered over with a thin layer of plaster, on which the pictorial representation was then painted.

The brush drawing differs from the pen drawing by its greater variation in stroke width, and by the stroke itself, which sets in more smoothly and is altogether less severely bordered. Early brush drawings nonetheless show a striking connection with the technique of the pen drawing. The early examples of the 15th century completely follow the flow of contemporaneous pen drawings. Leonardo's or Dürer's pen drawings, with their short, waxing and waning stroke layers, refine the system of pen drawing; many 16th-century artists used a comparable technique. The brush drawing for chiaroscuro sheets on tinted paper was popular because Chinese white, the main vehicle of delineation in this method, is more easily applied with the brush than the pen and because the intended pictorial effect is more easily attained, thanks to the possibility of changing abruptly to a plane representation.

Such representations are particularly distinctive as done by Vittore Carpaccio and Palma il Giovane in Venice and in a Mannerist spotting technique used by Parmigianino. In the 16th century, the brush nevertheless played a greater role as a supporting than as an independently form-giving instrument. Pure brush drawings were rare even in the 17th century, although the brush played a major role in landscapes, in which, by tinting of varying intensity, it ideally fulfilled the need to provide for all desired degrees of spatial depth and strength of lighting. Dutch artists, such as Adriaen Brouwer, Adriaen van Ostade, and Jan Steen, as well as the French artist Claude Lorrain, transcended the limits of drawing in the narrower meaning of the term by doing brushwork limited to a few tones within a monochrome scale, giving the impression of a pictorial watercolour.

Although the colouristically inclined 18th century was little interested in the restriction to a few shadings within one colour value, Jean-Honoré Fragonard raised this technique to perfection, with all its possibilities of

Claude Lorraine (1600–82) gave the impression of a pictorial water-colour with his brush drawing in *Landscape with a River, a Herd of Cattle, and a Herdsman,* which was executed in pen and bistre wash.

sharply accented contours, soft delineation, delicate tones, and deep shadows. The brush drawings of the Spanish painter Francisco Goya must also be counted among the great achievements of this technique. In his strong plastic effects, the English painter George Romney made the most of the contrast between the white foundation and the broad brushstrokes tinted in varying intensities. Other English artists, among them Alexander Cozens, John Constable, and J.M.W. Turner, took advantage of the delicately graded pictorial possibilities for their landscape studies.

In the 19th century, the French artists Théodore Géricault, Eugène Delacroix, and Constantin Guys still followed the character of the brush drawing, even though it was already being replaced by the variegated watercolour and gouache painting, a method of painting with opaque colours that have been ground in water and mingled with a preparation of gum. In modern drawing, the brush has regained some importance as an effective medium for contrasting planes and as carrier of the theme; in this, the dry brush has proven itself a useful tool for the creation of a granular surface structure.

COMBINATIONS OF VARIOUS TECHNIQUES

The combination of various techniques plays a greater role in drawing than in all other art forms. Yet it is necessary, in the numerous drawings in which two or more mediums are involved, to distinguish between those in which the mediums were changed in the course of artistic genesis and those in which

CLAUDE LORRAIN

French artist Claude Lorrain (1600–1682), usually called simply Claude in English, is best known for, and one of the greatest masters of, ideal landscape painting, an art form that seeks to present a view of nature more beautiful and harmonious than nature itself. The quality of that beauty is governed by Classical concepts, and the landscape often contains Classical ruins and pastoral figures in Classical dress. The source of inspiration is the countryside around Rome–the Roman Campagna–a countryside haunted with remains and associations of antiquity. The practitioners of ideal landscape during the 17th century, the key period of its development, were artists of many nationalities congregated in Rome. Later the form spread to other countries. Claude, whose special contribution was the poetic rendering of light, was particularly influential, not only during his lifetime but, especially in England, from the mid-18th to the mid-19th century.

Claude's parents seem to have died when

he was 12 years old, and within the next few years he traveled south to Rome, where he was trained as an artist by Agostino Tassi, a landscapist and the leading Italian painter of illusionistic architectural frescoes. Tassi taught Claude the basic vocabulary of his art–landscapes and coast scenes with buildings and little figures–and gave him a lasting interest in perspective and, thus, in landscape painting.

In 1625, Claude left Tassi and went back to Nancy, the capital of Lorraine, where he worked for a year as assistant to Claude Deruet. In the winter of 1626–27, Claude returned to Rome and settled there permanently. In 1633, to further his career, Claude joined the painters' Academy of St. Luke.

No work by Claude survives from before 1627, and he probably did not take up landscape until after that date. His first dated work is *Landscape with Cattle and Peasants* (1629). In the early 1630s, he rose to fame. He did this partly on the basis of two or three series of landscape frescoes (all but one, a small frieze in the Crescenzi Palace at Rome, are now lost), but, according to Baldinucci, he achieved renown chiefly because of his skill

(CONTINUED ON THE NEXT PAGE)

(*CONTINUED FROM THE PREVIOUS PAGE*)

in representing "those conditions of nature which produce views of the sun, particularly on seawater and over rivers at dawn and evening." By about 1637, Claude had become the leading landscape painter in Italy.

In 1635–36 he began the *Liber Veritatis* ("Book of Truth"; in the British Museum, London), a remarkable volume containing 195 drawings carefully copied by Claude after his own paintings, with particulars noted on the backs of the drawings indicating the patron for whom, or the place for which, the picture was destined, and, in the second half of the book, the date. Although most paintings executed before 1635 and a few executed afterward are not included, the *Liber Veritatis* was compiled throughout in chronological order and thus forms an invaluable record of Claude's artistic development, as well as revealing his circle of patrons. Undertaken, as he told Baldinucci, as a safeguard against forgery of his paintings, the book gradually became Claude's most precious possession and a work of art in itself; he may also have used it as a stock of motifs for new compositions.

About 250 paintings by Claude, out of a total of perhaps 300, and more than 1,000 drawings have survived. He also produced 44 etchings.

Claude's drawings are as remarkable an achievement as his paintings. About half are studies from nature. Executed freely in chalk or pen and wash, they are much more spontaneous than his paintings or studio drawings and represent informal motifs–trees, ruins, waterfalls, parts of a riverbank, fields in sunlight–that Claude saw on his sketching expeditions in the Campagna. Many were executed in bound books, which have since been broken up. The studio drawings consist partly of preparatory designs for paintings–Claude prepared his work more carefully than any previous landscape artist–and partly of compositions created as ends in themselves.

an artistic effect based on a combination of mediums was intended from the beginning.

In the first case, one is confronted with a preliminary sketch, as it were, of the eventual drawing: the basic structure with some variations is tried out in charcoal, chalk, metalpoint, pencil, or some other (preferably dry and easily corrected) material and then carried out in a stronger and more durable medium. Most pen drawings are thus superimposed on a preliminary sketch. The different materials actually represent two separate stages of the same artistic process.

More relevant artistically is the planned combination of different techniques that are meant to complement each other. The most significant combination from the stylistic point of view is that of pen and brush, with the pen delineating the contours that denote the object and the brush providing spatial and plastic as well as pictorial—that is, colour—values. The simplest combined form is manuscript illumination, where the delineated close contours are filled in with colour. The drawing may actually be improved if this is done by a hand other than the draftsman's or at a later time.

More important is brushwork that supplements linear drawing, in which entire segments may be given over to one technique or the other; for example, the considerable use of white (which is hard to apply with the pen) in drawings on tinted paper. In similar complementary fashion the brush may be used for plastic modeling as a way of highlighting, that is indicating the spots that receive the greatest illumination. The technique of combined pen-and-brush drawing was favoured by the draftsmen of Germany and the Netherlands, especially in the circle around Dürer and the south German Danube School. Shadows, too, can be inserted in a drawing with dark paint. The illusion of depth can also be achieved with white and dark colours in a pure chalk technique.

In contrast to these methods, which still belong to a linear system of drawing, is the flat differentiation of individual segments of a work in (usually)

the same medium: wash. Various bodies and objects
are evenly tinted with the brush within or along the
drawn contours. Planes are thus contrasted with
lines, enhancing the illusionary effect of plasticity,
space, and light and shadow. This modeling wash
has been used again and again since the 16th
century, sometimes in combination with charcoal,
chalk, or pencil drawings. A further refinement, used
particularly in landscape drawings, is wash in varying intensities; additional shadings in the sense of
atmospheric phenomena, such as striking light and
haze merging into fog and cloud, can be rendered
through thinning of the colour or repeated covering
over a particular spot. A chromatic element entered
drawing with the introduction of diluted indigo, known
in the Netherlands from the East India trade; it is
not tied to objects but used in spatial and illusionist
fashion, by Paul Brill and Hans Bol in the 16th and
17th centuries, for example. The mutual supplemen-
tation and correlation of pen and brush in the wash
technique was developed most broadly and consis-
tently in the 17th century, in which the scaffold, so to
speak, of the pen drawing became lighter and more
open, and brushwork integrated corporeal and spatial zones. The transition from one technique to the
other—from wash pen drawings to brush drawings
with pen accents—took place without a break. Claude
Lorrain and Nicolas Poussin in 16th- and 17th-cen-
tury France are major representatives of the latter
technique, and Rembrandt once again utilized all its
possibilities to the full.

Whereas this method served—within the general
stylistic intentions of the 17th century—primarily to

elucidate spatial and corporeal proportions, the artists of the 18th century employed it to probe this situation visually with the aid of light. The unmarked area, the spot left empty, has as much representational meaning as the pen contours, the lighter or darker brush accent, and the tinted area.

The art of omission plays a still greater role, if possible, in the later 19th century and in the 20th. Paul Cézanne's late sheets, with their sparse use of the pencil and the carefully measured out colour nuances, may be considered the epitome of this technique. As the colouring becomes increasingly varied through the use of watercolours to supplement a pen or metalpoint drawing, one leaves the concept of drawing in the strict sense of the term. According to the quality and quantity of the mediums employed, one then speaks of "drawings with watercolour," "watercolourized drawings," and "watercolours on preliminary drawings." The predominant stroke character, rather than the fact that paper is the carrier, is the chief feature when deciding whether or not the work may legitimately be called a drawing.

The combination of dry and fluid drawing mediums provides a genuine surface contrast that may be exploited for sensuous differentiation. Here again a distinction must be made between various ways of applying the identical medium—for example, charcoal and charcoal dust in a water solution or, more frequently, sanguine and sanguine rubbed in with a wet brush—and the stronger contrast brought about by the use of altogether different mediums. Chalk drawings are frequently washed with bistre or watercolour, after the principle of the washed pen drawing.

Stronger contrasts, however, can be obtained if the differing techniques are employed graphically, as the Flemish draftsmen of the 17th century liked to do. The Chinese ink wash of chalk drawings also contributes to the illusion of spatial depth. Along with such Dutch painters as Jan van Goyen and members of the family van de Velde, Claude Lorrain achieved great mastery in this technique. The differentiated treatment of the foreground with pen and brush and the background with chalk renders spatial depth plausible and plastic. In modern art, the use of different mediums—whether for plastic differentiation, such as Henry Moore carried out with unequalled mastery in his "Shelter Drawings," or only for the purpose of contrasting varied surface stimuli of nonrepresentational compositions as well as the enrichment with colours and even with collage elements (the addition of paper, metal, or other actual objects) broadens the concept of the drawing so that it becomes an autonomous picture the mixed technique of which transcends the borderline between drawing and painting.

MECHANICAL DEVICES

Mechanical aids are far less important for art drawing than for any other art form. Many draftsmen reject them altogether as unartistic and inimical to the creative aspect of drawing.

Apart from the crucial importance that mechanical aids have had and continue to have for all kinds of construction diagrams, plans, and other applied drawings, some mechanical aids have been used in varying

CAMERA OBSCURA

The camera obscura is an ancestor of the photographic camera. The Latin name means "dark chamber," and the earliest versions, dating to antiquity, consisted of small darkened rooms with light admitted through a single tiny hole. The result was that an inverted image of the outside scene was cast on the opposite wall, which was usually whitened. For centuries the technique was used for viewing eclipses of the Sun without endangering the eyes and, by the 16th-century, as an aid to drawing; the subject was posed outside and the image reflected on a piece of drawing paper for the artist to trace. The 17th-century camera obscura created an image by allowing light rays to enter a box through a small opening that was sometimes fitted with a focusing tube and lens. Owing to the device's limited depth of field, the image it projected would have many unfocused areas surrounded by hazy highlights. Dutch artist Johannes Vermeer (1632–75) was apparently fascinated by these optical effects, and he exploited them to give his paintings a greater sense of immediacy. Portable versions were built, followed by smaller and even pocket models; the interior of the box was painted black and the image reflected by an angled mirror so that it could be viewed right side up. The introduction of a light-sensitive plate by J.-N. Niepce created photography.

Children watch an outdoor scene through a camera obscura in 1887.

but significant measure for artistic drawings. The ruler, triangle, and compass as basic geometric instruments have played a major role, especially in periods in which artists created in a consciously constructionist and perspectivist manner. Marks for perspective constructions may be seen in many drawings of early and High Renaissance vintage.

For perspectively correct rendition, the graticulate frame, marked off in squares to facilitate proportionate enlargement or reduction, allowed the object to be drawn to be viewed in line with a screen on the drawing surface. Fixed points can be marked with relative ease on the resultant system of coordinates. For portrait drawings, the glass board used into the 19th century had contours and important interior reference points marked on it with grease crayons or soap sticks, so that they could be transferred onto paper by tracing or direct copying. Both processes are frequently used for preliminary sketches for engravings to be duplicated, as is the screened transmission of a preliminary sketch onto the engraving plate or, magnifying, the painting surface. In such cases the screen lies over the preparatory drawing.

Mirrors and mirror arrangements with reducing convex mirrors or concave lenses were likewise used (especially in the 17th and 18th centuries) as drawing aids in the preparation of reproductions. Even when it was a matter of the most exact rendition of topographical views, such apparatus, as well as the camera obscura (a darkened enclosure having an aperture usually provided with a lens through which light from external objects enters to form an image on the opposite surface), were frequently employed. In a darkened room the desired section is reflected through a lens onto a slanting mirror and from that inverse image is reflected again onto the horizontally positioned drawing surface. Lateral correction can be obtained by means of a second mirror.

Unless the proportions do not allow it, true-to-scale reducing or enlarging can also be carried out with the aid of the tracing instrument called the pantograph. When copying, the crayon or pencil inserted in the unequally long feet of the device reproduces the desired contours on the selected scale.

Most of these aids were thus used in normal studio practice and for the preparation of certain applied drawings. Equally practical, but useful only for closely circumscribed tasks, were elliptic compasses, curved rulers, and stencils, particularly for ornamental and decorative purposes. Only a few present-day artists, notably Jasper Johns, use stencils or simple blocks with a given shape in larger scale composition, in order to obtain the effect of repetition, often in an arbitrary use, in "alienating" technique and colour.

Mechanically produced drawings—such as typewriter sketches, computer drawings, oscillograms—and drawings done with the use of a projector, all of which can bring forth unusual and attractive results, nevertheless do not belong to the topic because they lack the immediate creativity of the art drawing.

THE CONSERVATION AND RESTORATION OF PRINTS AND DRAWINGS ON PAPER

The term *art conservation* denotes the maintenance and preservation of works of art and their protection from future damage and deterioration. *Art restoration,* by contrast, denotes the repair or renovation of artworks that have already sustained injury or decay and the attempted restoration of such objects to something approaching their original undamaged appearance.

Prints, drawings, and manuscripts have been created in many cultures over the centuries, with prints often tied to traditions of book illustration. Despite variables of media and forms of printing, a defining characteristic of prints and drawings is the way in which colorants such as inks, washes, pencils, and pastels become incorporated into the absorbent, fibrous texture of paper. Unlike paintings on canvas, which are laminated structures with distinct layers, even hard-pressed and heavily sized papers seize ink and colour; art on paper is a kind of amalgam, in which paper and pigment become inseparable. The permanence of prints and drawings is thereby greatly influenced by the quality of the paper support and by the environmental circumstances under which the artworks are housed. Despite being considered a fragile or ephemeral material, good-quality paper that receives proper handling and environmental stability has been known to survive for over one thousand years. Countless modern masterpieces have been made with inferior papers containing wood pulp, fugitive media, or poor technique, however. These qualities identify works with "inherent vice," and there is little the art conservator can do but provide the best possible environment to slow the inevitable deterioration of such works.

Most conservation treatments of prints and drawings or archives on paper aim to reduce the discolorations and acidity brought about by unfavourable climatic and storage conditions. These are commonly caused by contact with poor-quality acidic framing materials, matte-burn due to proximity to acidic window or back mattes, darkening due to light exposure and chemical deterioration, and brown spots known as "foxing," which may result from the combined influence of metallic particles in paper and mold. Additionally, attack on the cellulose and sizing of paper and paint media by biological pests such as silverfish, book lice, beetle larvae, mold, or fungus can result in very destructive and unsightly damages. The absorbent nature of paper renders it especially vulnerable to chemical transfer or image offset during storage, and so storage and framing with only acid-free archival papers (preferably 100 percent rag content) is generally the museum standard. Careful human handling, including prudent policy management for exhibition, ranks high among the factors influencing length of preservation of artworks on paper.

In terms of remedial treatment for deteriorated art on paper, there are numerous techniques and specialized equipment available to the paper conservator, including vacuum-suction tables, humidity chambers and platens, semipermeable plastic sheeting, steam and hot-air pencils, and leaf-casting apparatus. The conservator limits the use of moisture in procedures such as washing and stain reduction based on the degree of tolerance of the individual drawing media and on the subtle qualities of the paper. Immersion in water baths is limited to the most stable situations. Prudent use of bleaching, deacidification, and other reagents depend upon myriad circumstances, including the long-term aging characteristics after treatment and the possible consequences of residues left in the paper.

Repairs of mechanical damages to prints and drawings such as tears, thinning, or losses can be remedied by applying reinforcements, new paper inserts, or pulp into damaged areas. Additional overall support can be provided by adhering new paper (or backing sheet) to the reverse of the original. Typically, Japanese tissues, pure paper pulps, archival papers, and stable antique papers, used in combination with wheat- and rice-starch pastes, can be used for this purpose.

APPLIED DRAWINGS

Applied and technical drawings (also called drafting) differ in principle from art drawings in that they record unequivocally an objective set of facts and on the whole disregard aesthetic considerations.

TECHNICAL DRAWINGS

The contrast to the art drawing is sharpest in the case of technical project drawings, the purpose of which is to convey not so much visual plausibility as to give exact information that makes possible the realization of an idea. Such plans for buildings, machines, and technical systems are not instantly readable because of the orthogonal (independent) projection, the division into separate planes of projection, and the use of symbols. Prepared as a rule with such technical aids as ruler and compass, they represent a specialized language of their own, which must be learned.

ARCHITECTURAL DRAWINGS

At the design stage, both freehand and technical drawings serve the functions of inspiring and guiding the architect, builder, and collaborators. At this stage exact

A PANTOGRAPH

A pantograph is an instrument for duplicating a motion or copying a geometric shape to a reduced or enlarged scale. It consists of an assemblage of rigid bars adjustably joined by pin joints; as the point of one bar is moved over the outline to be duplicated, the motion is translated to a point on another bar, which makes the desired copy according to the predetermined scale. In the figure (below) the links 2, 3, 4, and 5 are connected by pin joints at O, A, B, and C. Joint O is fixed to a support, while joints A, B, and C are free to move. Link 5 is a solid bar continuing on to Q. Point P is the guided point and is usually fixed on link 4. As P is guided on

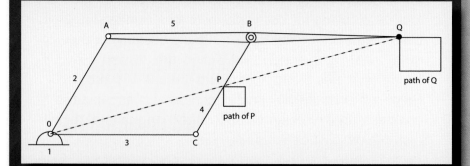

A pantograph is an instrument used for manually copying a figure to scale.

a specific path, such as the square in the Figure, point Q will follow a similar path on an enlarged scale. Conversely, if point Q is guided, point P will follow a similar path on a reduced scale.

The links in a pantograph may be arranged in other ways, but they all contain a parallelogram. Pantographs are used for reducing or enlarging engineering drawings and maps and for guiding cutting tools over complex paths. Artists specializing in miniatures use pantographs to achieve greater detail.

technical drawings can clarify, confirm, or disqualify a scheme that looked promising in a freehand sketch. Actually, both the sketch and the exact technical drawing are essential parts of the process of designing, and both belong to the field of drafting. After the basic design has been established, drafting skills aid in the development and transmission of the wealth of data necessary for the building's structure and construction. For a skyscraper tens of thousands of drawings may be needed to convey all of the requirements of the finished product from the designers to the fabricators.

The completion of the set of drawings necessary for the construction of a project involves three important factors: (1) itemization of every detail and requirement of the final product or project; (2) application of good judgment and knowledge of standard drafting procedures to select the combination of drawings and specifications that will convey the information identified in stage (1) in the clearest possible manner; and (3) deployment of skilled personnel and suitable equipment to produce the documents specified in stage (2).

Drafting is based on the concept of orthographic projection, which in turn is the principal concern of the branch of mathematics called descriptive geometry. Although preceded by the publication of related material and followed by an extensive development, the book *Géométrie descriptive* (1798) by Gaspard Monge, an 18th-century French mathematician, is regarded as the first exposition of descriptive geometry and the formalization of orthographic projection. The growth and development of the drafting profession were favoured by the application of the concepts published by Monge, the need to manufacture interchangeable parts, the introduction of the blueprinting process, and the economy offered by a set of drawings that in most cases made the building of a working model unnecessary.

Persons with a variety of skills and specialties are essential to the design and implementation of engineering and architectural projects. Drafting provides communication among them and coordination of their activities. The designer has primary responsibility for the basic conception and final solution but depends upon the support of several levels of drafters who prepare graphic studies of details; determine fits, clearances, and manufacturing feasibility; and prepare the working drawings. The delineator, or technical illustrator, converts preliminary or final drawings into pictorial representations, usually perspective constructions in full colour to help others visualize the product, to inform the public, to attract investment, or to promote sales. Before undertaking their own drawings, persons entering the profession of drafting may trace drawings to revise or repair them, then advance to the preparation of detail drawings, tables of materials, schedules of subassemblies (such as doors and windows), and the dimensioning of drawings initiated by more experienced colleagues. The wide spectrum of activities demanded of a design team requires that its members combine experience and creativity with skills in visualization, analysis, and delineation and with knowledge of materials, fabrication processes, and standards.

It is the responsibility of the manufacturing, fabricating, or construction workers to follow a set of drawings and specifications exactly; there should be no need for them to ask questions or make decisions regarding particulars of the design. All such particulars are the responsibility of the design team; the drawings must clearly convey all necessary information so that the functional requirements of and regulatory restrictions on the completed product or project are satisfied, the mechanical properties of the materials are appropriate, and the machining operations and assembly or erection procedures are possible.

Varying according to the product or project, the set of drawings generally contains detail drawings (also called working drawings), assembly drawings, section drawings, plans (top views), and elevations (front views). For manufacturing a machine, the shape and size of each individual part, except standard fasteners, are described in a detail drawing, and at least one assembly drawing indicates how the parts fit together. To clarify interior details or the fitting together of parts, it may be necessary to prepare a section drawing, showing a part or assembly as though it had been cut by a plane, with a portion of the object removed. For constructing a building, plans, elevations, section drawings, and

LOUIS SULLIVAN

American architect Louis Sullivan (1856–1924) is regarded as the spiritual father of modern American architecture and identified with the aesthetics of early skyscraper design. His more than 100 works in collaboration (1879–95) with Dankmar Adler include the Auditorium Building, Chicago (1887–89); the Guaranty Building, Buffalo, New York (1894–95; now Prudential Building); and the Wainwright Building, St. Louis, Missouri (1890–91). Frank Lloyd Wright apprenticed for six years with Sullivan at the firm. In independent practice from 1895, Sullivan designed the Schlesinger & Mayer department store (1898–1904; now the Sullivan Center) in Chicago. His *Autobiography* was published shortly before he died.

Sullivan was a spokesman for the reform of architecture, an opponent of historical eclecticism, and did much to remake the image of the architect as a creative personality. His own designs are characterized by richness of ornament. His importance lies in his writings as well as in his architectural achievements. These writings, which are subjective and metaphorical, suggest directions for architecture, rather than explicit doctrines or programs. Sullivan himself warned of the danger of mechanical theories of art.

Sources of Sullivan's ideas have been traced to the mid-19th-century writings of two Americans, the sculptor Horatio Greenough and the essayist Ralph Waldo Emerson, as well as to the English naturalist Charles Darwin. Darwin's writings on evolution, particularly on organic growth, left their mark on European writers on architecture and, in turn, on Sullivan's own thinking. The French architect César-Denis Daly, for example, in an essay reprinted in a Chicago architectural journal, stated that

> each style of architecture...being born of the intellectual and moral forces of a human society..., has become naturally the expression of a certain civilization... The adoption by one age of a style... other than that which it has itself created, is hence in itself a false principle.

Out of such inquiries into the nature of style came Sullivan's own famous dictum "form follows function," a phrase that should not lead one to conclude that Sullivan believed that a design should be a mechanistic visual statement of utility. Rather, he believed that architecture must evolve from and express the environment in addition to expressing its particular function and its structural basis. It has been said that Sullivan was the first American architect to think consciously of the relationship between architecture and civilization.

(CONTINUED ON THE NEXT PAGE)

(CONTINUED FROM THE PREVIOUS PAGE)

The skyscraper was central to both Sullivan's writing and his practice, and it is on this subject that his thought is most concise. His pre-skyscraper commercial buildings in Chicago, such as the Rothschild Store and the Troescher Building, show a conscious clarification and opening up of the facade. This simplification is carried into his "skyscrapers," the Wainwright and the Guaranty, which are conceived as "a single, germinal impulse or idea" that permeates "the mass and its every detail with the same spirit." The exceptional clarity of Sullivan's designs has lost some of its impact because contemporary architecture has in part absorbed his ideas. Sullivan considered it obvious that the design of a tall office building should follow the functions of the building and that, where the function does not change, the form should not change. Unfortunately, Sullivan's most dramatic skyscraper design, the Fraternity Temple (1891), intended for Chicago, was never built. This was to be a symmetrical structure with bold step-back forms and a soaring 35-story central tower.

Sullivan was just as much a revolutionary in his ornament as he was in his use of plain surfaces and cubic forms. His ornament was not based on historical precedent but rather upon geometry and the stylized forms of nature. Although his early ornament has some links to that of the Gothic Revival style and to the Queen Anne style, his mature ornament, seen best in his works at the turn of the century, is indisputably his own. It stands as a curious yet unrelated parallel to Art Nouveau ornamentation in Europe. Crisp yet fluid, tightly constructed yet exuberant, these designs remind one of Sullivan's feeling that architecture should not only serve and express society but also illuminate the heart.

detail drawings are necessary to convey the information needed to estimate costs and then erect the structure. In this case the detail drawings contain exact information about such features as elevators, stairways, cabinetwork, and the framing of windows, doors, and spandrels.

TOPOGRAPHIC AND CARTOGRAPHIC DRAWINGS

For topographic (detailed delineation of the features of a place) and cartographic (map-making) drawings, too, a special terminology has developed that above all systematizes spatial representations, making them intelligible to the expert with the aid of emblems and symbols.

SCIENTIFIC ILLUSTRATIONS

Equally far removed from any claim to artistic standing are most illustrations serving scientific purposes, the aim of which is to record as objectively as possible the characteristic and typical features of a given phenomenon. The systematic drawings, used especially in the natural sciences to explain a system or a function, resemble plans; descriptive and naturalistic illustrations, on the other hand, approach the illusionistic plausibility of visual experience and can attain an essentially artistic character. A good many artists have drawn scientific illustrations, and their works—the botanical and zoological drawings of the Swiss Merian family in the 17th and 18th centuries, for example—are today more esteemed for their artistic than for their documentary value.

JOHN JAMES AUDUBON

John James Audubon (1785–1851) was an ornithologist, artist, and naturalist who became particularly well known for his drawings and paintings of North American birds.

Young Audubon developed an interest in drawing birds during his boyhood in France. At age 18 he was sent to the United States to avoid conscription and to enter business. He began his study of North American birds at that time; this study would eventually lead him from Florida to Labrador, Canada. With Frederick Rozier, Audubon attempted to operate a mine and then a general store. The latter venture they attempted first in Louisville, Kentucky, and later

This illustration of a Great Blue Heron appeared in John James Audubon's *Birds of America* (1827–38) and was based on his drawing.

(CONTINUED ON THE NEXT PAGE)

(CONTINUED FROM THE PREVIOUS PAGE)

in Henderson, Kentucky, but the partnership was dissolved after they failed utterly. Audubon then attempted some business ventures in partnership with his brother-in-law; these too failed. By 1820 he had begun to take what jobs he could to provide a living and to concentrate on his steadily growing interest in drawing birds; he worked for a time as a taxidermist and later made portraits and taught drawing.

By 1824 he had begun to consider publication of his bird drawings, but he was advised to seek a publisher in Europe, where he would find better engravers and greater interest in his subject. In 1826 he went to Europe in search of patrons and a publisher. He was well received in Edinburgh and, after the king subscribed to his books, in London as well. The engraver Robert Havell of London undertook publication of his illustrations as The *Birds of America*, 4 vol. (435 hand-coloured plates, 1827–38). William MacGillivray helped write the accompanying text, *Ornithological Biography,* 5 vol. (octavo, 1831–39), and *A Synopsis of the Birds of North America* (1839), which serves as an index. Until 1839 Audubon divided his time between Europe and the United States, gathering material, completing illustrations, and financing publication through subscription. His reputation established, Audubon then settled in New York City and prepared a smaller edition of his *Birds of America*, 7 vol. (octavo, 1840–44), and a new work, *Viviparous Quadrupeds of North America*, 3 vol. (150 plates, 1845–48), and the accompanying text (3 vol., 1846–53), completed with the aid of his sons and the naturalist John Bachman.

Critics of Audubon's work have pointed to certain fanciful (or even impossible) poses and inaccurate details, but few argue with its excellence as art. To many, Audubon's work far surpasses that of his contemporary (and more scientific) fellow ornithologist Alexander Wilson.

ILLUSTRATIVE DRAWINGS

Of a similarly ambivalent nature is the illustrative drawing that perhaps does not go beyond a simple pictorial rendition of a literary description but because of its specific formal execution may still satisfy the highest artistic demands.

ILLUSTRATIONS

Great artists have again and again illustrated Bibles, prayer books, novels, and literature of all kinds. Some of the famous examples are Botticelli's illustrations for Dante's *Divine Comedy* and Dürer's marginal illustrations for the emperor Maximilian's prayer book. Some artists have distinguished themselves more as illustrators than as autonomous draftsmen, as for example the 18th-century German engraver Daniel Chodowiecki, the 19th-century caricaturist Honoré Daumier, the

SCRATCHBOARD

Scratchboard, also called Scraperboard, is a technique used by commercial artists and illustrators to make drawings that can easily be reproduced and that closely resemble either wood engravings or woodcuts. Introduced in the 19th century, the process involves the use of a specially prepared board coated with a ground of chalk and glue or some similar absorbent substance, such as gesso. Textured boards with a prepared pattern or stippling are also available. The artist coats the board evenly with black drawing ink and works on it by scraping away with special tools, known as "scratch knives," those lines or surfaces he wants to appear white on the finished work. Corrections can easily be made by reapplying ink and then reworking the surface.

Alternatively, if the artist wants to create the effect of a woodcut, as opposed to wood engraving, he removes

A scratchboard illustration depicts daffodils, periwinkle, and Easter eggs.

large areas of ink and leaves the lines and surfaces appearing black-on-white. Essentially designed as a reproductive medium, scratchboard is rarely used to produce single, nonrepetitive drawings.

19th-century satiric artist Wilhelm Busch, and the 20th-century Austrian illustrator Alfred Kubin.

CARICATURE

Clearly connected with illustrative drawing is caricature, which, by formally overemphasizing the characteristic traits of a person or situation, creates a suggestive picture that—precisely because of its distortion—engraves itself on the viewer's mind. This special kind of drawing was done by such great artists as Leonardo, Dürer, and the 17th-century artist Gian Lorenzo Bernini and by draftsmen who, often for purposes of social criticism, have devoted themselves wholly to caricaturing, such as the 18th-century Italian Pier Leone Ghezzi, the 19th-century Frenchman Grandville (professional name of Jean-Ignace-Isidore Gérard), the 19th-century American political cartoonist Thomas Nast, and the 20th-century American Al Hirschfeld.

CARTOONS

From such overdrawn types developed continuous picture stories that could dispense to a considerable

AL HIRSCHFELD

Al Hirschfeld (1903–2003) was an American caricature artist, especially known for his drawings appearing in *The New York Times*, portraying show-business personalities.

Hirschfeld's family moved from St. Louis, Missouri, to upper Manhattan in New York City when he was 11, and at age 17 he went to work as the art director of Selznick Studios in the city's Astoria district. With money saved, he went to Europe in 1924 to study art, residing mostly in Paris in the 1920s but returning often to New York City. In 1925 a Hirschfeld caricature drawn on a theatre Playbill was reproduced by *The New York Herald Tribune*. After his work became more popular and was published in several New York newspapers, he entered into an agreement with *The New York Times* in 1929 for the use of his theatre caricatures, and his drawings appeared in the newspaper up until his death. Following the birth of his daughter, Nina, he began hiding her name in the drawings and it became something of a pastime for readers to discover how many times her name appeared. (His work of theatrical and nontheatrical personalities continued to appear in numerous other publications.) In the 1930s he took a long trip to the Far East, where Japanese and Javanese art is said to have influenced his graphic style.

Al Hirschfeld holds up a caricature at his desk in his New York City studio in 1985.

Beginning in the 1940s, Hirschfeld illustrated books by such authors as S.J. Perelman (*Westward Ha!* [1948], *Swiss Family Perelman* [1950]), Fred Allen (*Treadmill to Oblivion* [1954]), and Brooks Atkinson (*The Lively Years* [1973]); and he also began producing books of which he was both author and illustrator, such as *Show Business Is No Business* (1951) and *Hirschfeld by Hirschfeld* (1979). In *The World of Hirschfeld* (1968) he wrote extensively about his life and technique. Hirschfeld's drawings, watercolours, lithographs, etchings, and sculptures are to be found in both private and museum collections. Although his caricatures were noted for their wit, Hirschfeld was not malicious, and it became something of an honour to be drawn by him.

extent with the explanatory text. Modern cartoons are based on these picture stories. Through the formally identical treatment of peculiar types, these drawings acquire an element of consecutiveness that, by telling a continuing story, adds a temporal dimension to two-dimensional drawing. This element is strongest in trick drawings that fix on paper, in brief segments of move-ment, invented creatures and phenomena that lack all logical plausibility; a rapid sequence of images (leafing through the pages, seeing it projected on the screen) turns the whole into apparent motion, the fundamen-tal process of animation. The artistic achievement, if any, lies in the original invention; its actual realization is predetermined and sometimes carried out by a large and specialized staff of collaborators, often with the aid of stencils and traced designs. Moreover, since the final result is partially determined by the mechanical multi-plication, an essential criterion of drawing—the unity of work and result—does not apply.

CHAPTER FOUR

SUBJECT MATTER

Anything in the visible or imagined universe may be the theme of a drawing. In practice, however, by far the greatest number of art drawings in the Western world deal with the human figure. This situation springs from the close bond between drawing and painting: in sketches, studies, and compositions, drawing prepared the way for painting by providing preliminary clarification and some formal predetermination of the artist's concept of a given work. Many drawings now highly regarded as independent works were originally "bound," or "latent," in that they served the ends of

Mary Cassatt drew portraits of mothers and their children, such as *Maternal Kiss* (1897), and genre pictures in pastels.

painting or sculpture. Yet, so rounded, self-contained, and aesthetically satisfying are these drawings that their erstwhile role as handmaidens to the other pictorial arts can be reconstructed only from knowledge of the completed work, not from the drawing itself. This situation is especially true of a pictorial theme that acquired, at a relatively early stage, an autonomous rank in drawing itself: the portrait.

PORTRAITS

Drawn 15th-century portraits—by Pisanello or Jan van Eyck, for example—may be considered completed pictorial works in their concentration, execution, and distribution of space. The clear, delicately delineated representation follows every detail of the surface, striving for realism. The profile, rich in detail, is preferred; resembling relief, it is akin to the medallion. Next in prominence to the pure profile, the three-quarter profile, with its more spatial effect, came to the fore, to remain for centuries the classic portrait stance.

The close relationship to painting applies to practically all portrait drawings of the 15th century. Even so forceful a work as Dürer's drawing of the emperor Maximilian originated as a portrait study for a painting. At the same time, however, some of Dürer's portrait drawings clearly embody the final stage of an artistic enterprise, an ambivalence that can also be observed in other 16th-century portraitists. The works of Jean and François Clouet in France and of the younger Hans Holbein in Switzerland and even more markedly in England in the same century bestowed an autonomy

Jan van Eyck made this detailed and realistic preparatory drawing of *The Portrait of Cardinal Nicola Albergati*, c. 1431, in silverpoint before he painted it in oil.

on portrait drawing, especially when a drawing was completed in chalk of various colours. The choice of the softer medium, the contouring, which for all its exactitude is less severely self-contained, and the more delicate interior drawing with plane elements gives these drawings a livelier, more personal character and accentuates once more their proximity to painting.

In polychromatic chalk technique and pastel, portrait drawing maintained its independence into the 19th century. In the 18th-century, Quentin de La Tour, François Boucher, and Jean-Baptiste Chardin—all of these artists from France—were among its chief practitioners, and even Ingres, living in the 19th century, still used its technique. In pastel painting, the portrait outweighed all other subjects.

In the choice of pose, type, and execution, portrait painting, like other art forms, is influenced by the general stylistic features of an epoch. Thus, the extreme pictorial attitude of the late Baroque and Rococo was followed by a severer conception during Neoclassicism, which preferred monochrome techniques and cultivated as well the special form of the silhouette, a profile contour drawing with the area filled in in black. Unmistakably indebted to their 15th-century predecessors, the creators of portrait drawings of the early 19th century aimed once more at the exact rendition of detail and plastic effects gained through the most carefully chosen graphic mediums: the thin, hard pencil was their favourite instrument, and the silverpoint, too, was rediscovered by the Romantics.

More interested in the psychological aspects of portraiture, late 19th- and 20th-century draftsmen preferred the softer crayons that readily follow every artistic impulse. The seizing of characteristic elements and an adequate plane rendition weighed more heavily with them than realistic detail. Mood elements, intellectual tension, and personal engagement are typical features of the modern portrait and thus also of modern portrait drawing, an art that continues to document the artist's personal craftsmanship beyond the characteristics of various techniques.

HANS HOLBEIN THE YOUNGER

Hans Holbein the Younger (1497/98–1543) was a German painter, draftsman, and designer, renowned for the precise rendering of his drawings and the compelling realism of his portraits, particularly those recording the court of King Henry VIII of England.

Holbein was a member of a family of important artists. His father, Hans Holbein the Elder, and his uncle Sigmund were renowned for their somewhat conservative examples of late Gothic painting in Germany. One of Holbein's brothers, Ambrosius, became a painter as well, but he apparently died about 1519 before reaching maturity as an artist. The Holbein brothers no doubt first studied with their father in Augsburg; they both also began independent work about 1515 in Basel, Switzerland.

(CONTINUED ON THE NEXT PAGE)

(CONTINUED FROM THE PREVIOUS PAGE)

Han Holbein the Younger's precise rendering of poet Sir Thomas Wyatt, c. 1535–37, was drawn with chalk and pen and ink.

It should be noted that this chronology places Holbein firmly in the second generation of 16th-century German artists. Albrecht Dürer, Matthias Grünewald, and Lucas Cranach the Elder all were born between 1470 and 1480 and were producing their mature masterpieces by the time Holbein was just beginning his career. Holbein is, in fact, the only truly outstanding German artist of his generation.

Holbein's work in Basel during the decade of 1515–25 was extremely varied, if also sometimes derivative. Trips to northern Italy (c. 1517) and France (1524) certainly affected the development of his religious subjects and portraiture, respectively. Holbein entered the painters' corporation in 1519, married a tanner's widow, and became a burgher of Basel in 1520. By 1521 he was executing important mural decorations in the Great Council Chamber of Basel's town hall.

Holbein was associated early on with the Basel publishers and their humanist circle of acquaintances. There he found portrait commissions such as that of the humanist scholar Bonifacius Amerbach (1519). In this and other early portraits, Holbein showed himself to be a master of the current German portrait idiom, using robust characterization and accessories, strong gaze, and dramatic silhouette. In portraiture, Holbein's minute sense of observation

(CONTINUED ON THE NEXT PAGE)

(CONTINUED FROM THE PREVIOUS PAGE)

was soon evident. His first major portrait of Desiderius Erasmus (1523) portrays the Dutch humanist scholar as physically withdrawn from the world, sitting at his desk engaged in his voluminous European correspondence; his hands are as sensitively rendered as his carefully controlled profile.

Protestantism, which had been introduced into Basel as early as 1522, grew considerably in strength and importance there during the ensuing four years. By 1526 severe iconoclastic riots and strict censorship of the press swept over the city. In the face of what, for the moment at least, amounted to a freezing of the arts, Holbein left Basel late in 1526, with a letter of introduction from Erasmus, to travel by way of the Netherlands to England. Though only about 28 years old, he would achieve remarkable success in England. His most impressive works of this time were executed for the statesman and author Sir Thomas More and included a magnificent single portrait of the humanist (1527). In this image, the painter's close observation extends to the tiny stubble of More's beard, the iridescent glow of his velvet sleeves, and the abstract decorative effects of the gold chain that he wears. Holbein also completed a life-size group portrait of More's family; this work is now lost, though its appearance is preserved in copies and in preparatory drawing. This painting was the first example in northern European art of a large group portrait in which the figures are not shown kneeling–the effect of which is to suggest the individuality of the sitters rather than impiety.

Before Holbein journeyed to England in 1526, he had apparently designed works that were both pro- and anti-Lutheran in character. On returning to Basel in 1528, he was admitted, after some hesitation, to the new–and now official–faith. It would be difficult to interpret this as a very decisive change, for Holbein's most impressive religious works, like his portraits, are brilliant observations of physical reality but seem never to have been inspired by Christian spirituality. This is evident in both the claustrophobic, rotting body of the *Dead Christ in the Tomb* (1521) and in the beautifully composed *Family of Burgomaster Meyer Adoring the Virgin* (1526). In this latter painting, Holbein skillfully combined a late medieval German compositional format with precise Flemish realism and a monumental Italian treatment of form. Holbein apparently quite voluntarily gave up almost all religious painting after about 1530.

In Basel from 1528 to 1532, Holbein continued his important work for the town council. He also painted what is perhaps his only psychologically penetrating portrait, that of his

(CONTINUED ON THE NEXT PAGE)

wife and two sons (c. 1528). This picture no doubt conveys some of the unhappiness of that abandoned family. In spite of generous offers from Basel, Holbein left his wife and children in that city for a second time, to spend the last 11 years of his life primarily in England.

By 1533 Holbein was already painting court personalities, and four years later he officially entered the service of King Henry VIII of England. He died in a London plague epidemic in 1543. It is estimated that during the last 10 years of his life Holbein executed approximately 150 portraits, life-size and miniature, of royalty and nobility alike. These portraits ranged from a magnificent series depicting German merchants who were working in London to a double portrait of the French ambassadors to Henry VIII's court (1533) to portraits of the king himself (1536) and his wives Jane Seymour (1536) and Anne of Cleves (1539). In these and other examples, the artist revealed his fascination with plant, animal, and decorative accessories. Holbein's preliminary drawings of his sitters contain detailed notations concerning jewelry and other costume decorations as well. Sometimes such objects point to specific events or concerns in the sitter's life, or they act as attributes referring to a sitter's occupation or character. The relation between accessories and face is a charged and stimulating one that avoids simple correspondence.

In an analogous fashion, Holbein's mature portraits present an intriguing play between surface and depth. The sitter's outlines and position within the frame are carefully calculated, while inscriptions applied on the surface in gold leaf lock the sitter's head into place. Juxtaposed with this finely tuned two-dimensional design are illusionistic miracles of velvet, fur, feathers, needlework, and leather. Holbein acted not only as a portraitist but also as a fashion designer for the court. The artist made designs for all the state robes of the king; he left, in addition, more than 250 delicate drawings for everything from buttons and buckles to pageant weapons, horse outfittings, and bookbindings for the royal household. This choice of work indicates Holbein's Mannerist concentration on surface texture and detail of design, a concern that in some ways precluded the incorporation of great psychological depth in his portraits.

Holbein was one of the greatest portraitists and most exquisite draftsmen of all time. It is the artist's record of the court of King Henry VIII of England, as well as the taste that he virtually imposed upon that court, that was his most remarkable achievement.

LANDSCAPES

As early as the 15th century, landscape drawings, too, attained enough autonomy so that it is hard to distinguish between the finished study for the background of a particular painting and an independent, self-contained sketched landscape. Already in Jacopo Bellini's 15th-century sketchbooks (preserved in albums in the British Museum and the Louvre), there is an intimate connection between nature study and pictorial structure; in Titian's studio in the 16th century, landscape sketches must have been displayed as suggestions for pictorial backgrounds.

Albrecht Altdorfer drew *Sarmingstein on the Danube*, 1511, as a true landscape in which the scene of nature, river, and town was meant to be the theme of the artwork.

But it was Dürer who developed landscape as a recollected image and autonomous work of art, in short, as a theme of its own without reference to other works. His watercolours above all but also the drawings of his two Italian journeys, of the surroundings of Nürnberg, and of the journey to the Netherlands, represent the earliest pure landscape drawings. Centuries had to pass before such drawings occurred again in this absolute formulation.

Landscape elements were also very significant in 16th-century German and Dutch drawings and illustrations. The figurative representation, still extant in most cases, is formally quite integrated into the romantic forest-and-meadow landscape, particularly in the works of the Danube School—Albrecht Altdorfer and Wolf Huber, for example. More frequently than in other schools, one finds here carefully executed nature views. In the Netherlands, Pieter Bruegel drew topographical views as well as free landscape compositions, in both cases as autonomous works.

In the 17th century, the nature study and the landscape drawing that grew out of it reached a new high. The landscape drawings of the Accademia degli Incamminati (those of Domenichino, for example) combined classical and mythological themes with heroic landscapes. The Frenchman Claude Lorrain, living in Rome, frequently worked under the open sky, creating landscape drawings with a hitherto unattained atmospheric quality. This type of cultivated and idealized landscape, depicted also by Poussin and other Northerners residing in Rome (they were called Dutch Romanists in view of the fact that so many artists from the Netherlands lived in Rome, their drawings of Italy achieving an almost ethereal quality), is in contrast with

THE DANUBE SCHOOL

The Danube School, in German called *Donauschule*, was a tradition of landscape painting that developed in the region of the Danube River valley in the early years of the 16th century.

A number of painters are considered to have been members of the Danube school. Chief among them was the Regensburg master Albrecht Altdorfer (c. 1480–1538), whose real subject, although he often included figures in his compositions and gave some of his paintings religious titles, was nature; he saw man's presence in nature as more or less incidental. Altdorfer's interest in the changes caused by light at different times of the day and the changes of the seasons of the year, as well as the continuous cycle of growth, decay, and rebirth, link him spiritually with both Baroque and the 19th-century Romantic landscapists.

The early works of Lucas Cranach (1472–1553) are also typical of the Danube landscape style. Altdorfer's landscapes can be characterized as poetic and enchanting, whereas Cranach's were expressive and dramatic in contrast. In Cranach's work the mood of nature has been adjusted to complement the subject.

Other important artists of this school include the Austrian Wolf Huber and the German Jorg Breu the Elder. Some of Wolf Huber's most expressive and poetic works are his landscapes, for example, the drawings he made of the Danube River valley on a trip (c. 1529) from Passau to Vienna.

the unheroic, close-to-nature concept of landscape held primarily by the Netherlanders when depicting the landscape of their native country. All landscape painters—their landscape paintings a specialty that was strongly represented in the artistically specialized Low Countries—also created independent landscape drawings (Jan van Goyen and Jacob van Ruisdael, for example), with Rembrandt again occupying a special position: capturing the characteristics of a region often with only a few strokes, he enhanced them in such manner that they acquire monumental expressive power even in the smallest format. In 18th-century Italy, the topographically faithful landscape drawing gained in importance with the advent of the Vedutisti, the purveyors of "views," forming a group by themselves (among them, Giambattista Piranesi and Canaletto [Giovanni Antonio Canal]) and often working with such optical aids as the graticulate frame and camera obscura. Landscape drawings of greater artistic freedom, as well as imaginary landscapes, were done most successfully by some French artists, among them Hubert Robert; pictorially and atmospherically, these themes reached a second flowering in the brush-drawn landscapes of such English artists as J.M.W. Turner and Alexander Cozens, whose influence extends well into the 20th century.

Given their strong interest in delineation, the 18th-century draftsmen of Neoclassicism and, even more, of Romanticism observed nature with topographical accuracy. As a new "discovery," the romantically and heroically exaggerated Alpine world now took its place in the artist's mind alongside the arcadian view of the Italian landscape.

Landscape drawings and even more, watercolours, formed an inexhaustible theme in the 19th century. The French artist Jean-Baptiste-Camille Corot and, toward the end of the century, Cézanne and van Gogh, were among the chief creators of landscape drawings. Landscapes formed part of the work of many 20th-century draftsmen, but, for much of the century, the genre as such took second place to general problems of form, in which the subject was treated merely as a starting point. However, during the last 30 years of the 20th century, a large number of American artists returned to representation, thus reinvesting in the land-scape as a subject.

FIGURE COMPOSITIONS AND STILL LIFES

Compared to the main themes of autonomous draw-ing—portraiture and landscape—all others are of lesser importance. Figure compositions depend greatly on the painting of their time and are often directly connected with it. There were, to be sure, artists who dealt in their drawings with the themes of monumental painting, such as the 17th-century engraver and etcher Raymond de La Fage; in general, however, the artistic goal of figure composition is the picture, with the drawing representing but a useful aid and a way station. Genre scenes, especially popular in the 17th-century Low Countries (as done by Adriaen Brouwer, Adriaen van Ostade, and Jan Steen, for example) and in 18th-century France and England, did attain some independent standing. In the 19th century, too, there were drawings that told stories of everyday life; often illustrative in character, they may be called "small pictures," not only on account of the frequently multicoloured format but also in their artistic execution.

Still lifes can also lay claim to being autonomous drawings, especially the representations of flowers, such as those of the Dutch artist Jan van Huysum, which have been popular ever since the 17th century. Here, again, it is true that a well-designed arrangement transforms an immediate nature study into a pictorial composition. In some of these compositions the similarity to painting is very strong; the pastels of the 19th- and 20th-century artist Odilon Redon, for instance, or the work of the 20th-century German Expressionist Emil Nolde, with its chromatic intensity, transcend altogether the dividing line between drawing and painting. In still lifes, as in landscapes, autonomous principles of form are more important to modern artists than the factual statement.

ODILON REDON

Odilon Redon (1840–1916) was a French Symbolist painter, lithographer, and etcher of considerable poetic sensitivity and imagination, whose work developed along two divergent lines. His prints explore haunted, fantastic, often macabre themes and foreshadowed the Surrealist and Dadaist movements. His oils and pastels, chiefly still lifes with flowers, won him the admiration of Henri Matisse and other painters as an important colourist.

Redon studied under Jean-Léon Gérôme; mastered engraving from Rodolphe Bresdin, who exerted an important influence; and learned lithography under Henri Fantin-Latour. His aesthetic was one of imagination rather than visual perception. His imagination found an intellectual catalyst in his close friend, the Symbolist poet Stéphane Mallarmé. Redon was also associated with the group of Symbolist painters.

Redon produced nearly 200 prints, beginning in 1879 with the lithographs collectively titled *In the Dream*. He completed another series (1882) dedicated to Edgar Allan Poe, whose poems had been translated into French with great success by Mallarmé and Charles Baudelaire. Rather than illustrating Poe, Redon's lithographs are poems in visual terms, themselves evoking the poet's world of private torment. There is an evident link to Goya in Redon's imagery of winged demons and menacing shapes, and one of his series was the *Homage to Goya* (1885).

About the time of the print series *The Apocalypse of St. John* (1889), Redon began devoting himself to painting and colour drawing—sensitive floral studies, and heads that appear to be dreaming or lost in reverie. He developed a unique palette of powdery and pungent hues. Though there is a relationship between his work and that of the Impressionist painters, he opposed both Impressionism and Realism as wholly perceptual.

FANCIFUL AND NONREPRESENTATIONAL DRAWINGS

Drawings with imaginary and fanciful themes are more independent of external reality. Dream apparitions, metamorphoses, and the entwining of separate levels and regions of reality have been traditional themes. The late 15th-century phantasmagoric works of Hieronymus Bosch are an early example. There are allegorical peasant scenes by the 16th-century Flemish artist Pieter

Bruegel and the carnival etchings of the 17th-century French artist Jacques Callot. Others whose works illustrate what can be done with drawing outside landscape and portraiture are: the 18th-century Italian engraver Giovanni Battista Piranesi, the 18th-century Anglo-Swiss artist Henry Fuseli, the 19th-century English illustrator Walter Crane, the 19th-century French Symbolist artist Gustave Moreau, and the 20th-century Surrealists.

WALTER CRANE

Although he was a distinguished craftsman, designer, and writer, Walter Crane (1845–1915) is best known for his imaginative illustrations of children's books, especially fairy tales.

Crane was born in Liverpool, England, the son of the portrait painter and miniaturist Thomas Crane. From 1859 to 1862 he served as an apprentice to the wood engraver W.J. Linton in London, where he was able to study both the Italian old masters and contemporary works. Probably the most important technical development in his art derived from his study of Japanese colour prints, whose methods he used in a series of toy books (1869–75), thereby starting a new fashion. The ideas and teachings of the artists known as the Pre-Raphaelites and of the artist and critic John Ruskin manifested themselves in his early paintings, such as *The Lady of Shalott* (1862). Crane came to oppose the policies of the traditional art establishment, which steadily refused to show his later work. In 1864 he began to illustrate an admirable series of inexpensive toy books of nursery rhymes for Edmund Evans, the colour printer. A new series, beginning with *The Frog Prince* (1873), was more elaborate, and to the Japanese influence was added that of Florentine 15th-century painting, following a long visit to Italy.

A strong moral element underlies much of Crane's work, and for several years he contributed weekly cartoons to the socialist periodicals *Justice* and *The Commonweal.* Many of these were collected as *Cartoons for the Cause* (1896). He was founder-president of the Art Workers' Guild and in 1888 founded the Arts and Crafts Exhibition Society. Crane designed Art Nouveau textiles and wallpaper that became internationally popular. He became art director first of the Manchester School of Art (1893–96), then of Reading College (1896–98), and finally principal of the Royal College of Art in London (1898–99).

Crane's chief importance lies in book illustration, the standard of which he helped greatly

(CONTINUED ON THE NEXT PAGE)

(CONTINUED FROM THE PREVIOUS PAGE)

to raise. He worked with William Morris in 1894 on the page decorations of *The Story of the Glittering Plain*, printed by the Kelmscott Press in the style of 16th-century German and Italian woodcuts. Among the best of his book illustrations are those for Edmund Spenser's *Faerie Queene* (1895–97) and *The Shepheardes Calendar* (1897).

·KING·COLE·

Walter Crane illustrated the whimsical "King Cole" from *Sing a Song of Sixpence*, c. 1865.

Nonrepresentational art, with its reduction of the basic elements of drawing—point, line, plane—to pure form, offered new challenges. Through renunciation of associative corporeal and spatial relationships, the unfolding of the dimensions of drawing and the structure of the various mediums acquire new significance. The graphic qualities of the line in the plane as well as the unmarked area had already been emphasized in earlier times—for example, in the grotteschi of Giuseppe Arcimboldo in the 16th century (the fanciful or fantastic representations of human and animal forms often combined with each other and interwoven with representations of foliage, flowers, fruit, or the like) and in calligraphic exercises such as moresques (strongly stylized linear ornament, based on leaves and blossoms)—but mostly as printing or engraving models for the most disparate decorative tasks (interior decoration, furniture, utensils, jewelry, weapons, and the like).

ARTISTIC ARCHITECTURAL DRAWINGS

There is one field in which drawing fulfills a distinct function: artistic architectural drawings are a final product as drawings, differing from the impersonal, exact plans and

Piranesi embellished the building's scale in *The Smoking Fire*, 1761, to magnify its dramatic qualities.

GIOVANNI BATTISTA PIRANESI

Giovanni Battista Piranesi (1720–1778) was an Italian draftsman, printmaker, architect, and art theorist. His large prints depicting the buildings of classical and postclassical Rome and its vicinity contributed considerably to Rome's fame and to the growth of classical archaeology and to the Neoclassical movement in art.

At the age of 20 Piranesi went to Rome as a draftsman for the Venetian ambassador. He studied with leading printmakers of the day and settled permanently in Rome in 1745. It was during this period that he developed his highly original etching technique, producing rich textures and bold contrasts of light and shadow by means of intricate, repeated bitings of the copperplate.

He created about 2,000 plates in his lifetime. The "Prisons" (*Carceri*) of about 1745 (some were reissued in 1761) are his finest early prints; they depict ancient Roman or Baroque ruins converted into fantastic, visionary dungeons filled with mysterious scaffolding and instruments of torture. Among his best mature prints are the series *Le Antichità romane* (1756; "Roman Antiquities"), the *Vedute di*

Roma ("Views of Rome"; appearing as single prints between 1748 and 1778), and the views of the Greek temples at Paestum (1777–78). His unparalleled accuracy of depiction, his personal expression of the structures' dramatic and romantic grandeur, and his technical mastery made these prints some of the most original and impressive representations of architecture to be found in Western art.

designs by the same "handwriting" character that typifies art drawings. In many cases, no execution of these plans was envisaged; since the early Renaissance, such ideal plans have been drawn to symbolize, in execution and accessories, an abstract content. Despite the often considerable exactitude with which the plans are drawn, the personal statement predominates in the flow of the line. This personal note clearly identifies the drawings of such artists and architects as Albrecht Altdorfer, Leonardo, Michelangelo, Bernini, Francesco Borromini, and Piranesi.

Also distinct from the ground-plan type of architectural drawing are the art drawings of autonomous character created by such 20th-century architects as Erich Mendelsohn and Le Corbusier.

THE HISTORY OF DRAWING

As an artistic endeavour, drawing is almost as old as mankind. In an instrumental, subordinate role, it developed along with the other arts in antiquity and the Middle Ages.

WESTERN HISTORY

Whether preliminary sketches for mosaics and murals or architectural drawings and designs for statues and reliefs within the variegated artistic production of the Gothic medieval building and artistic workshop, drawing as a nonautonomous auxiliary skill was subordinate to the other arts. Only in a very limited sense can one speak of centres of drawing in the early and High Middle Ages; that is, the scriptoria of the monasteries of Corbie and Reims in France, as well as those of Canterbury and Winchester in England, and also a few places in southern Germany, where various strongly delineatory (graphically illustrated) styles of book illumination were cultivated.

THE 14TH, 15TH, AND 16TH CENTURIES

In the West, the history of drawing as an independent artistic document began toward the end of the 14th century. If its development was independent, however, it was not insular. Just as the greatest draftsmen have been for the most part also distinguished painters, illustrators, sculptors, or architects, so the centres and the high points of drawing have generally coincided with the leading localities and the major epochs of the other arts. Moreover, the same stylistic phenomena have been expressed in drawing as in other art forms. Indeed, drawing shares with other art forms the characteristics of individual style, period style, and regional features. Drawing differs, however, in that it interprets and

Jacopo Bellini's *Adoration of the Magi*, c.1450, a pen and ink drawing on vellum, is a sheet from Bellini's album of highly finished drawings now at the Louvre. Another album of his drawings is held in the British Museum.

renders these characteristics in terms of its own unique mediums.

Drawing became an independent art form in northern Italy, at first quite within the framework of ordinary studio activity. But with nature studies, copies of antiques, and drafts in the various sketchbooks (those of Giovannino de'Grassi, Antonio Pisanello, and Jacopo Bellini) the tradition of the Bauhütten studio workshop changed to individual work: the place of "exempla," models, reproduced in formalized fashion was now being taken by subjectively probing and partially creative drawings. In the early 15th century the international Soft style of the period still largely predominated over the draftsman's individual "handwriting." At mid-century, however, the differentiation of drawing style according to region and the artist's personality set in. Essential criteria, destined to remain characteristic for generations, begin to strike the eye.

In drawing produced north of the Alps, the characteristic features lie in the tendency to pictorial compactness and precise execution of detail. Many painters produced individual drawings, but the most notable draftsmen are the otherwise unidentified 15th-century German Master of the Housebook and his contemporary Martin Schongauer. Both of these artists were also major copperplate engravers, so that it is not always easy to determine whether the work is a preliminary sketch or an independent drawing.

In Italian Renaissance drawings, of which there are a great many, the diverging stylistic features of the various artistic regions were particularly evident. What they had in common was the overwhelming importance of the sketch and the study, in contrast to the far rarer finished drawings. The formal and thematic connection

JACOPO BELLINI

Jacopo Bellini (c. 1400–c. 1470) was a painter who introduced the principles of Florentine early Renaissance art into Venice.

He was trained under the Umbrian artist Gentile da Fabriano, and in 1423 he had accompanied his master to Florence. There the progress made in fidelity to nature and in mastery of classic grace by such masters as Donatello and Ghiberti, Masaccio and Paolo Uccello offered Jacopo further inspiration.

By 1429 Jacopo was settled at Venice and had established himself as the city's most important painter. The use of gold pigment in highlights of such works as his *Madonna* (c. 1438; Accademia, Venice) shows that Jacopo long retained elements derived from Byzantine art, while the Child's rich robes and the patterned background of angels reveal his continued interest in the higher decorative style in which he was trained, conventionally called International Gothic. The modeling of the figures, the confident rendering of folds of cloth, and the accurate perspective, however, indicate an excellent understanding of the progressive art of 15th-century Florence. In the life-sized *Crucifixion* (Museo di Castelvecchio, Verona),

(CONTINUED ON THE NEXT PAGE)

(CONTINUED FROM THE PREVIOUS PAGE)

the spare and sombre scene strictly conforms to the Florentine Renaissance style of Masaccio and repudiates the rich colouring and courtly grace of Bellini's earlier known works.

More important than his paintings are his two books of drawings (c. 1450). The Louvre in Paris and the British Museum in London each own one of these sketchbooks. The drawings depict a great variety of scenes, and artists used them as models for compositions well into the 16th century. In such drawings as the *Nativity*, the *Flagellation*, and *St. John the Baptist Preaching*, Jacopo experimented with linear perspective and was among the first to make figures diminish in space using rules of perspective formerly applied only to depictions of architecture. The *Crucifixion* (British Museum, London) is among Jacopo's boldest compositional experiments. Possibly for the first time in art, the three crosses are viewed at an angle instead of frontally, and the soldiers' backs are turned to the viewer, lending a spontaneity and immediacy rare in Italian art of the time. Jacopo's great influence upon Venetian art was heightened through the work of his sons, Gentile and Giovanni, and his son-in-law, Andrea Mantegna, all of whom were prominent painters in the vicinity of Venice.

with painting is very close even when it was not a question of preliminary drawings. The draftsmen of Venice and northern Italy preferred an open form with loose and interrupted delineation in order to achieve even in drawing the pictorial effect that corresponded to their painters' imagination.

In central Italy, on the other hand, and especially in Florence, it was the clear contour that predominated, the closed and firmly circumscribed form, the static and plastic character. Corresponding to the functional purpose of drawing, the individual artists' studios (which, as was the case with the Medicis' Academy of St. Mark, also had to engage in general educational and humanistic investigations) formed the most significant centres of art drawing. In these large studios, drawing served not only for the probing realization of creative ideas, it was not only study and mediator between the conception and the master's finished work; it functioned also as teaching aid for the assistants who worked with the master and as a vehicle for the formation and preservation of an individual workshop tradition. Although Leonardo's scientific interests were expressed in a large number of drawings, his ideal concept of the human figure is much more frequently preserved in the drawings of his collaborators and successors than in his own. Raphael and Michelangelo were also outstanding draftsmen. Each of them used drawing in order to allow his thoughts about individual works to mature; each had a highly personal drawing style, the one with a soft and rounded stroke, the other with a sculptor's intermittent and powerful stroke. Probably a great deal of drawing was done in Raphael's studio, especially if only for the preparation of the engravings after Raphael's compositions. From Michelangelo's hand came the first so-called

LEONARDO DA VINCI'S NOTEBOOKS AND ANATOMICAL STUDIES

Leonardo da Vinci (1452–1519) was an Italian painter, draftsman, sculptor, architect, and engineer whose genius, perhaps more than that of any other figure, epitomized the Renaissance humanist ideal. His notebooks reveal a spirit of scientific inquiry and a mechanical inventiveness that were centuries ahead of their time.

In the years between 1490 and 1495, the great program of Leonardo the writer (author of treatises) began. During this period, Leonardo's interest in two fields—the artistic and the scientific—developed and shaped his future work, building toward a kind of creative dualism that sparked his inventiveness in both fields. He gradually gave shape to four main themes that were to occupy him for the rest of his life: a treatise on painting, a treatise on architecture, a book on the elements of mechanics, and a broadly outlined work on human anatomy. His geophysical, botanical, hydrological, and aerological researches also began in this period and constitute parts of the "visible cosmology" that loomed before him as a distant goal. He scorned speculative book knowledge, favouring instead the irrefutable facts gained from experience—from *saper vedere* ("knowing how to see").

From this approach came Leonardo's far-reaching concept of a "science of painting." Leon Battista Alberti and Piero della Francesca had already offered proof of the mathematical basis of painting in their analysis of the laws of perspective and proportion, thereby buttressing his claim of painting being a science. But Leonardo's claims went much further: he believed that the painter, doubly endowed with subtle powers of perception and the complete ability to pictorialize them, was the person best qualified to achieve true knowledge, as he could closely observe and then carefully reproduce the world around him. Hence, Leonardo conceived the staggering plan of observing all objects in the visible world, recognizing their form and structure, and pictorially describing them exactly as they are.

It was during his first years in Milan that Leonardo began the earliest of his notebooks. He would first make quick sketches of his observations on loose sheets or on tiny paper pads he kept in his belt; then he would arrange them according to theme and enter them in order in the notebook. Surviving in notebooks from throughout his career are a first collection of material for a painting treatise, a model book of sketches for sacred and profane architecture, a treatise on elementary theory of mechanics, and the first sections of a treatise on the human body.

(CONTINUED ON THE NEXT PAGE)

(CONTINUED FROM THE PREVIOUS PAGE)

Leonardo's notebooks add up to thousands of closely written pages abundantly illustrated with sketches—the most voluminous literary legacy any painter has ever left behind. Of more than 40 codices mentioned—sometimes inaccurately—in contemporary sources, 21 have survived; these in turn sometimes contain notebooks originally separate but now bound so that 32 in all have been preserved. To these should be added several large bundles of documents: an omnibus volume in the Biblioteca Ambrosiana in Milan, called *Codex Atlanticus* because of its size, was collected by the sculptor Pompeo Leoni at the end of the 16th century; after a roundabout journey, its companion volume fell into the possession of the English crown in the 17th century and was placed in the Royal Library in Windsor Castle. Finally, the *Arundel Manuscript* in the British Museum in London contains a number of Leonardo's fascicles on various themes.

One special feature that makes Leonardo's notes and sketches unusual is his use of mirror writing. Leonardo was left-handed, so mirror writing came easily and naturally to him—although it is uncertain why he chose to do so. While somewhat unusual, his script can be read clearly and without difficulty with the help of a mirror—as his contemporaries testified—and should not be looked on as a secret handwriting. But the fact that Leonardo used mirror writing throughout the notebooks, even in his copies drawn up with painstaking calligraphy, forces one to conclude that, although he constantly addressed an imaginary reader in his writings, he never felt the need to achieve easy communication by using conventional handwriting. His writings must be interpreted as preliminary stages of works destined for eventual publication that Leonardo never got around to completing. In a sentence in the margin of one of his late anatomy sketches, he implores his followers to see that his works are printed.

Another unusual feature in Leonardo's writings is the relationship between word and picture in the notebooks. Leonardo strove passionately for a language that was clear yet expressive. The vividness and wealth of his vocabulary were the result of intense independent study and represented a significant contribution to the evolution of scientific prose in the Italian vernacular. Despite his articulateness, Leonardo gave absolute precedence to the illustration over the written word in his teaching method. Hence, in his notebooks, the drawing does not illustrate the text; rather, the text serves to explain the picture. In formulating his own principle of graphic representations—which he called *dimostrazione* ("demonstrations")—Leonardo's work was a precursor of modern scientific illustration.

In defining painting as a science, Leonardo also emphasizes its mathematical basis. In

(CONTINUED ON THE NEXT PAGE)

(*CONTINUED FROM THE PREVIOUS PAGE*)

the notebooks he explains that the 10 optical functions of the eye ("darkness, light, body and colour, shape and location, distance and closeness, motion and rest") are all essential components of painting. He addresses these functions through detailed discourses on perspective that include explanations of perspectival systems based on geometry, proportion, and the modulation of light and shade. He differentiates between types of perspective, including the conventional form based on a single vanishing point, the use of multiple vanishing points, and aerial perspective. In addition to these orthodox systems, he explores–via words and geometric and analytic drawings–the concepts of wide-angle vision, lateral recession, and atmospheric perspective, through which the blurring of clarity and progressive lightening of tone is used to create the illusion of deep spatial recession. He further offers practical advice–again through words and sketches–about how to paint optical effects such as light, shadow, distance, atmosphere, smoke, and water, as well as how to portray aspects of human anatomy, such as human proportion and facial expressions.

Leonardo's fascination with anatomical studies reveals a prevailing artistic interest of the time. It cannot be determined exactly when Leonardo began to perform dissections, but it might have been several years after he first moved to Milan, at the time a centre of medical investigation. His study of anatomy, originally pursued for his training as an artist, had grown by the 1490s into an independent area of research. As his sharp eye uncovered the structure of the human body, Leonardo became fascinated by the *figura istrumentale dell' omo* ("man's instrumental figure"), and he sought to comprehend its physical working as a creation of nature. Over the following two decades, he did practical work in anatomy on the dissection table

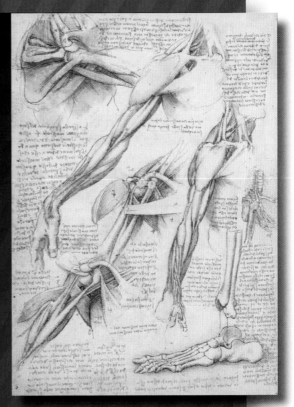

Leonardo drew these studies of the muscles of the right shoulder and arm, and bones of the left foot and leg in about 1510–11.

in Milan, then at hospitals in Florence and Rome, and in Pavia, where he collaborated with the physician-anatomist Marcantonio della Torre. By his own count Leonardo dissected 30 corpses in his lifetime.

Leonardo's early anatomical studies dealt chiefly with the skeleton and muscles; yet even

(CONTINUED ON THE NEXT PAGE)

(CONTINUED FROM THE PREVIOUS PAGE)

at the outset, Leonardo combined anatomical with physiological research. From observing the static structure of the body, Leonardo proceeded to study the role of individual parts of the body in mechanical activity. This led him finally to the study of the internal organs; among them he probed most deeply into the brain, heart, and lungs as the "motors" of the senses and of life. His findings from these studies were recorded in the famous anatomical drawings, which are among the most significant achievements of Renaissance science. The drawings are based on a connection between natural and abstract representation; he represented parts of the body in transparent layers that afford an "insight" into the organ by using sections in perspective, reproducing muscles as "strings," indicating hidden parts by dotted lines, and devising a hatching system. The genuine value of these *dimostrazione* lay in their ability to synthesize a multiplicity of individual experiences at the dissecting table and make the data immediately and accurately visible; as Leonardo proudly emphasized, these drawings were superior to descriptive words. The wealth of Leonardo's anatomical studies that have survived forged the basic principles of modern scientific illustration. It is worth noting, however, that during his lifetime, Leonardo's medical investigations remained private. He did not consider himself a professional in the field

of anatomy, and he neither taught nor published his findings.

Although he kept his anatomical studies
to himself, Leonardo did publish some of his
observations on human proportion. Working
with the mathematician Luca Pacioli, Leonardo
considered the proportional theories of
Vitruvius, the 1st-century BCE Roman architect,
as presented in his treatise *De architectura*
("On Architecture"). Imposing the principles of
geometry on the configuration of the human
body, Leonardo demonstrated that the ideal
proportion of the human figure corresponds
with the forms of the circle and the square.
In his illustration of this theory, the so-called
Vitruvian Man, Leonardo demonstrated that
when a man places his feet firmly on the
ground and stretches out his arms, he can be
contained within the four lines of a square, but
when in a spread-eagle position, he can be
inscribed in a circle.

Leonardo envisaged the great picture chart
of the human body he had produced through
his anatomical drawings and *Vitruvian Man* as *a
cosmografia del minor mondo* ("cosmography
of the microcosm"). He believed the workings of
the human body to be an analogy, in microcosm,
for the workings of the universe.

connoisseur drawings that are esteemed as a personal document. They are the precursors of the collector's drawings that began in the later 16th century (autonomous works, destined for collections).

North of the Alps the autonomy of drawing was championed in the first instance by Albrecht Dürer, an indefatigable draftsman who mastered all techniques and exercised an enduring and widespread influence. The delineatory constituent clearly predominates even in his paintings. They were distinguished by exquisite precision of detail. This corresponds to the general stylistic character of 16th-century German art, within which Matthias Grünewald, with his freer, broader, and therefore more pictorial style of drawing, and the painters of the Danube school, with their ornamentalizing and agitated stroke, represent significant exceptions. In their metamorphosing of the perceived reality into drawings, the landscapes of Albrecht Altdorfer and Wolf Huber in particular are astonishing documents of a feeling for nature that might almost be called Romantic. The medieval and Renaissance artists of Germany did their best work in engraving, woodcutting, and drawing. Between the mid-15th and mid-16th centuries, they surpassed all other artists in these fields. It is known that the prints of Martin Schongauer served as inspiration for Raphael and that they were admired by Michelangelo.

Soberer, incredibly compact in their pictorial concept and yet akin to the Renaissance in their objective viewing, were the portrait drawings of Hans Holbein the Younger, whose sojourns in 16th-century England proved stimulating to other artists as well. Similar, if less personal than Holbein because of the stricter linearity of their work, were the drawings of the French portraitists Jean and François Clouet. In the Low Countries, where they

François Clouet drew this portrait of Marguerite de Valois in chalk, c. 1559. Clouet immortalized the members of the court of the royal house of Valois in his precise and elegant portraits.

were combined with the idealized image of Italy (as in the drawings of Lucas van Leyden), Dürer's methods gained lasting popularity in the landscape drawings and studies "after life" by Pieter Bruegel the Elder.

Drawing acquired a pivotal significance in the period of Mannerism (c. 1525–1600), both as a document of artistic invention and as a means of its realization. Jacopo da Pontormo in Florence, Parmigianino in northern Italy, and Tintoretto in Venice used point and pen as essential and spontaneous vehicles of expression. Their drawings were clearly related to their painting, both in content and in the graphic method of sensitive contouring and daringly drawn foreshortening.

THE 17TH, 18TH, AND 19TH CENTURIES

In the early 17th century, Jacques Callot rose to prominence in French art: gifted as a draftsman above all, he recorded with the pen his clever inventions and great picture stories, primarily in bold abbreviations.

Jacque Callot etched *The Hangman's Tree* (from the series *The Miseries and Misfortunes of War*) in 1633. Callot depicted the destruction and savagery of the Thirty Years' War.

The importance of drawing for an artist's growth and the widening of his horizon is attested also by the work of Peter Paul Rubens, whose studies and sketches make up an integral part of his creative achievement. In order to disseminate his pictorial themes and concept of form, he maintained his own school for draftsmen and engravers. Among the circle of Flemings around him, Jacob Jordaens and Sir Anthony Van Dyck are notable as draftsmen with a style of their own.

JACQUES CALLOT

French printmaker Jacques Callot (1592–1635) was one of the first great artists to practice the graphic arts exclusively. His innovative series of prints documenting the horrors of war greatly influenced the socially conscious artists of the 19th and 20th centuries.

Callot's career was divided into an Italian period (c. 1609–21) and a Lorraine (France) period (from 1621 until his death). He learned the technique of engraving under Philippe Thomassin in Rome. About 1612 he went to Florence. At that time Medici patronage expended itself almost exclusively in *feste*, quasi-dramatic pageants, sometimes dealing in allegorical subjects, and Callot was employed to make pictorial records of these mannered, sophisticated entertainments. He succeeded

(CONTINUED ON THE NEXT PAGE)

(CONTINUED FROM THE PREVIOUS PAGE)

in evolving a naturalistic style while preserving the artificiality of the occasion, organizing a composition as if it were a stage setting and reducing the figures to a tiny scale, each one indicated by the fewest possible strokes. This required a very fine etching technique. His breadth of observation, his lively figure style, and his skill in assembling a large, jostling crowd secured for his etchings a lasting popular influence all over Europe.

Callot also had a genius for caricature and the grotesque. His series of plates of single or dual figures—for example, the *Balli di Sfessania* ("Dance of Sfessania"), the *Caprices of Various Figures*, and the *Hunchbacks*—are witty and picturesque and show a rare eye for factual detail.

With a few exceptions, the subject matter of the etchings of the Lorraine period is less frivolous, and Callot was hardly employed at all by the court at Nancy. He illustrated sacred books, made a series of plates of the Apostles, and visited Paris to etch animated maps of the sieges of La Rochelle and the Île de Ré. In his last great series of etchings, the "small" (1632) and the "large" (1633) *The Miseries and Misfortunes of War,* he brought his documentary genius to bear on the atrocities of the Thirty Years' War. Callot is also well known for his landscape drawings in line and wash and for his quick figure studies in chalk.

Hercules Seghers was among the most fascinating artists of the 17th century, a creator of drawn and etched landscapes that he continued to rework while experimenting with printing processes. From the point of view of technique and form, he was important for the greatest artist of Holland, Rembrandt. Seghers combined great inventiveness, especially in his interpretations of Old Testament motifs, and broad mastery of all the techniques of drawing. In his studio, too, drawing was emphasized as a teaching aid and a means of formal experimentation.

Most Dutch painters of the 17th century, such as the van de Velde family, Brouwer, van Ostade, Pieter Saenredam, and Paulus Potter, were also industrious draftsmen who recorded their special thematic concerns in drawings that were largely completed. Beyond serving as preparation for paintings, these were regarded as autonomous works representing the final stage of the creative process.

In 17th-century Italy, drawing by way of artistic practice and experimentation became established in the academies, especially in Bologna. More significant, however, was the continuing development of landscape drawing, as initiated by the brothers Agostino and Annibale Carracci and articulated further by Domenichino and Salvator Rosa. The French artist Claude Lorrain so developed the landscape drawing of the Roman countryside that it became almost a genre of its own; in his works, which were often intended for sale, nature study and an idealized pictorial concept are uniquely merged. In detailed studies directly before the object, he achieved a timeless validity. Like Lorrain, Nicolas Poussin also drew under the open sky. Using various techniques, he combined realistic experiences and humanistic concepts in idealizing compositions the figures and scenes of which are harmoniously integrated into a spacious landscape. This open-air painting and drawing was practiced also by some other artists who spent a considerable time in Rome—the Dutch artists Jan Asselijn, Claes Berchem, Karel Dujardin, and Adam Pijnacker, for example. For most southern European artists of the 17th century, however, drawing was a mere stage in the creation of a painting.

Antoine Watteau, too, did drawings to "keep his hand in" for his painting, although he did so with an independence that led him far beyond the immediate occasion. Most figures in the paintings from various periods of his career were based on earlier drawings. In the grand scale of his form and the attention paid to pictorial elements, he carried on in the manner of Rubens, combining it with the light esprit of the 18th century. The leading position of French art in the first half of that century was confirmed by the achievements of François Boucher, Jean-Honoré Fragonard, Hubert Robert, and Gabriel de Saint-Aubin, whose drawings include figure studies, genre-like works, and landscapes.

In contrast to the French draftsmen who brought about a flowering of the à trois crayons ("with three pencils") method on tinted paper, some artists created similar landscapes with pen and brush but with greater objective abbreviation. Mention must here be made of Venice, with the Giovanni Battista Tiepolo family, whose expansively conceived pen drawings, washed with a broad brush, call forth the kind of luminaristic effect that Francesco Guardi also used for landscape studies and imaginary scenes. These had been preceded by Canaletto's views of Venice, composed more severely as far as tectonic (constructional) detail is concerned but nonetheless the first examples of this form of the landscape capriccio, or fantasy. The architect Giovanni Battista Piranesi made his name primarily as a drafts-man who recorded views of Rome; above all, in his drawings of architecture and eerie vaults (*Carceri*), he left behind a body of work of great intellectual and for-mal forcefulness.

The Spanish painter Francisco de Goya, at the very end of the 18th and in the beginning of the 19th century, was in advance of his time in the way in which he handled his themes. Forming an odd contrast to the court-painter's pictures, his brush-and-sanguine drawings are rather more closely tied to his cycles of etchings. He combined the luminaristic effects of Tiepolo's drawings with the dramatic impact of a Rembrandt chiaroscuro.

Also at the turn of the 19th century is an artist whose main work was that of a draftsman: the English caricaturist and social satirist Thomas Rowlandson, who produced colourful and distinctive watercolours. The late 18th and, even more, the early 19th century pro-duced a drawing style that, in accordance with both the Neoclassical and the Romantic ideal, emphasized once more the linear element. In Jean-Auguste-Dominique Ingres, idealistic Neoclassicism found an exemplary expression of strict linearity, and the pencil drawing became a downright classical form. The Nazarenes and Romantics in Rome and the Alpine region (Joseph Anton Koch, the brothers Friedrich and Ferdinand Olivier, and Julius Schnorr von Carolsfeld) as well as those in north Germany (Philipp Otto Runge and Caspar David Friedrich) were more lyrical but equally rigorous in the use of the hardpoint; after a long time, they were

THOMAS ROWLANDSON

Thomas Rowlandson (1756–1827) was an English painter and caricaturist who illustrated the life of 18th-century England and created comic images of familiar social types of his day, such as the antiquarian, the old maid, the blowsy barmaid, and the Grub Street hack. His characters ranged from the ridiculously pretentious, with their elaborate coiffures, widely frogged uniforms, and enormous bosoms and bottoms, to the merely pathetic, whose trailing handkerchiefs expressed their dejected attitudes.

The son of a tradesman, Rowlandson became a student in the Royal Academy. At age 16 he went to study in Paris. After establishing a studio as a portrait painter, he began to draw caricatures to supplement his income, and this soon became his major interest.

His series of drawings "The Schoolmaster's Tour," accompanied by verses of William Combe, was published in the new *Poetical Magazine* (1809–11) launched by the art publisher Rudolph Ackermann, who was Rowlandson's chief employer. The same collaboration of designer, author, and publisher resulted in the popular Dr. Syntax series—*Tour of Dr. Syntax in Search of the Picturesque* (1812), *The Second Tour of Dr.*

Syntax in Search of Consolation (1820), and *The Third Tour of Dr. Syntax in Search of a Wife* (1821). They also produced *The English Dance of Death* (1815–16) and *The Dance of Life* (1816–17). Rowlandson illustrated editions of novels by Tobias Smollett, Oliver Goldsmith, and Laurence Sterne.

Rowlandson's designs were usually executed in outline with a reed pen and delicately washed with colour.

Thomas Rowlandson drew *Comet* in pencil, pen, ink, and watercolour in 1821. He made fun of people straining to watch a comet.

They were then etched by the artist on copper and afterward aquatinted—usually by a professional engraver, the impressions being finally coloured by hand. The works of Rowlandson's prime are outstanding in the vitality of their outline and the gusto of their comment on human weaknesses.

the first northern artists to have made a significant contribution to the history of drawing. Among 19th-century artists, the emphasis on delineation was characteristic also of Moritz von Schwind in Germany and John Millais in England. (In the Neoclassical phase of the 20th century it was renewed, in a more open and "handwriting" fashion, by Thomas Eakins in the United States as well as by Picasso, Matisse, and Amedeo Modigliani in France.) The drawings of Eugène Delacroix, while preserving plastic qualities, show a broader stroke and are thus more pictorial. Honoré Daumier, active in all mediums primarily as a draftsman, utilized pictorial chiaroscuro effects in forcible statements of social criticism.

France continued to be a leading centre of the art of drawing, a form that was given a very personal note in each case in the works of Edgar Degas, Henri de Toulouse-Lautrec, Vincent van Gogh, and Paul Cézanne. The line—the common point of departure for all of the above-mentioned artists—did not disappear until Georges Seurat's plane shading, done in the Pointillist manner.

EASTERN HISTORY

Some form of monochromatic brush drawing with ink may have been practiced in China as early as the 2nd millennium BCE; but the earliest pictorial work is in lacquer or on bronze vessels, contemporaneous with Alexander the Great (ruled 336–323 BCE). It relies on contour and silhouette, with men and animals depicted in horizontal registers (levels, one above the other) reminiscent of Egyptian and Mediterranean work. The extent of any mutual influence between East and West cannot yet be determined. Under the Eastern Han dynasty (25–220 CE) wall paintings, linear in character, were produced in fresco (wet plaster) and secco (dry). Only in the Wei (386–534/35) and Tang (618–907) dynasties did the true character of Chinese drawing on silk or paper emerge. In the 7th century, the characteristic albums (*ceye*) of drawings appear.

No distinction was made between drawing and painting because all Chinese pictorial art was fundamentally graphic. The artist worked with the fine point of the brush on paper or silk laid horizontally on a table. Work in pure outline was called *baimiao*; ink applied in splashes, *pomo*. Colour was used sparingly or not at all. The final work was not made direct from nature.

Hindu and Buddhist paintings at Ajanta in India and also in Sri Lanka reveal the essential quality in all Indian art: emphasis on a flowing, rhythmic contour to express

A detail from Huang Gongwang's ink and brushwork hand scroll *Dwelling in the Fuchun Mountains*, c. 1347–50, is considered by most scholars to be one of the greatest landscapes of the Yuan dynasty.

movement and gesture. Drawings on palm leaf of the 11th century are similarly based on the use of line to depict mythological scenes.

The 14th century saw the manufacture of paper, introduced from China, permitting the production of the vertical book. Despite the Muslim prohibition of human representation, books illustrated with drawings, sometimes with flat decorative colour, were produced at the Persian and Mughal courts, but not for public display. The use of a precise and expressive line constituted the basis for Persian and Indian (both Mughal and Rajput) miniature paintings, which show people in landscape or in relation to buildings.

HOKUSAI

Hokusai (1760–1849) was a Japanese master artist and printmaker of the ukiyo-e ("pictures of the floating world") school. His early works represent the full spectrum of ukiyo-e art, including single-sheet prints of landscapes and actors, hand paintings, and *surimono* ("printed things"), such as greetings and announcements. Later he concentrated on the classical themes of the samurai and Chinese subjects. His famous print series *Thirty-six Views of Mount Fuji*, published between 1826 and

1833, marked the summit in the history of the Japanese landscape print.

Hokusai was born in the Honjo quarter just east of Edo (Tokyo) and became interested in drawing at the age of five. He was adopted in childhood by a prestigious artisan family named Nakajima.

Hokusai is said to have served in his youth as clerk in a lending bookshop, and from 15 to 18 years of age he was apprenticed to a wood-block engraver. This early training in the book

Hokusai drew Chinese philosopher Laozi reading a scroll while riding on an ox, a symbol of spiritual strength and benevolence.

(CONTINUED ON THE NEXT PAGE)

(CONTINUED FROM THE PREVIOUS PAGE)

and printing trades obviously contributed to Hokusai's artistic development as a printmaker.

The earliest contemporary record of Hokusai dates from the year 1778, when, at the age of 18, he became a pupil of the leading ukiyo-e master, Katsukawa Shunshō. The young Hokusai's first published works appeared the following year—actor prints of the kabuki theatre, the genre that Shunshō and the Katsukawa school practically dominated.

To judge from the ages of his several children, Hokusai must have married in his mid-20s. Possibly under the influence of family life, from this period his designs tended to turn from prints of actors and women to historical and landscape subjects, especially *uki-e* (semi-historical landscapes using Western-influenced perspective techniques), as well as prints of children. The artist's book illustrations and texts turned as well from the earlier themes to historical and didactic subjects. At the same time, Hokusai's work in the *surimono* genre during the subsequent decade marks one of the early peaks in his career. *Surimono* were prints issued privately for special occasions—New Year's and other greetings, musical programs and announcements, private verse selections—in limited editions and featuring immaculate printing of the highest quality.

Hokusai's master Shunshō died early in 1793, and somewhat later Hokusai's young wife passed away, leaving a son and two daughters. In the year 1797 he remarried and adopted the name Hokusai. This change of name marks the beginning of the golden age of his work, which was to continue for a half century.

In format, Hokusai's oeuvre from this period covers the gamut of ukiyo-e art: single-sheet prints, *surimono*, picture books and picture novelettes, illustrations to verse anthologies and historical novels, erotic books and album prints, and hand paintings and sketches. In his subject matter, Hokusai only occasionally (in a few notable prints, in paintings, and erotica) chose to compete with Utamaro, the acknowledged master of voluptuous figure prints. Aside from this limitation, however, Hokusai's work encompassed a wide range, with particular emphasis on landscape views and historical scenes in which figures were often of secondary interest. Around the turn of the century he experimented for a time with Western-style perspective and colouring.

From the early 19th century Hokusai commenced illustrating *yomihon* (the extended historical novels that were just coming into fashion). Under their influence, his style began to suffer important and clearly visible changes between 1806 and 1807. His figure work becomes more powerful but increasingly less delicate; there is greater attention to classical or traditional themes (especially of samurai, or

(CONTINUED ON THE NEXT PAGE)

(CONTINUED FROM THE PREVIOUS PAGE)

warriors, and Chinese subjects) and a turning away from the contemporary *Ukiyo*-e world.

In about the year 1812, Hokusai's eldest son died. This tragedy was not only an emotional but also an economic event, for, as adopted heir to the affluent Nakajima family, the son had been instrumental in obtaining a generous stipend for Hokusai, so that he did not need to worry about the uncertainties of income from his paintings, designs, and illustrations, which at this period were paid for more with "gifts" than with set fees.

Whether for economic reasons or not, from this time on Hokusai's attention turned gradually from novel illustration to the picture book and, particularly, to the type of wood-block-printed copybook designed for amateur artists (including the famous *Hokusai manga*).

Though famed for his detailed prints and illustrations, Hokusai was also fond of displaying his artistic prowess in public–making, for example, huge paintings (some fully 200 square metres [about 2,000 square feet] in area) of mythological figures before festival crowds, in both Edo and Nagoya. He was once even summoned to show his artistic skills before the shogun (the military leader who, although theoretically subordinate to the emperor, was in fact the ruler of Japan).

In the summer of 1828, Hokusai's second wife died. The master was then 68, afflicted intermittently with paralysis and left alone, evidently with only a profligate grandson, who had proved to be an incorrigible delinquent. Hokusai's favourite daughter (and pupil), O-ei, broke her unhappy marriage with a minor artist named Tōmei and returned to her father's side, where she was to stay for his remaining years.

An energetic artist, Hokusai rose early and continued painting until well after dark. This was the customary regimen of his long, productive life. Of Hokusai's thousands of books and prints, his *Thirty-six Views of Mt. Fuji* is particularly notable. Published from about 1826 to 1833, this famous series (including supplements, a total of 46 colour prints) marked a summit in the history of the Japanese landscape print; in grandeur of concept and skill of execution there was little approaching it before and nothing to surpass it later—even in the work of Hokusai's famed late contemporary Hiroshige.

Hokusai embodied in his long lifetime the essence of the *Ukiyo*-e school of art during its final century of development. His stubborn genius also represents, in its 70 years of continuous artistic creation, the prototype of the single-minded artist, striving only to complete a given task. Moreover, Hokusai constitutes a figure who has, since the later 19th century, impressed Western artists, critics, and art lovers alike, more, possibly, than any other single Asian artist.

Japanese art tended to follow that of China until the early 19th century, when the popular colour print was introduced. In the graceful feminine gestures of Utamaro's work, the Eastern love of flowing contour is manifest, his lines varying in width and density. Hokusai's drawings of social life in a humorous, almost grotesque vein reveal his complete command of the expressive line.

Except for a few stylistic currents such as Tachism (paintings consisting of irregular blobs of colour), drawing is represented in the work of practically all 20th-century artists; it is as international as modern art itself. As the other arts have become non-representational, thus attaining autonomy and formal independence in relation to external reality, drawing is more than ever considered an autonomous work of art, independent of the other arts. Some schools and individual artists as well have concentrated on drawing and in very individualistic ways. The German Expressionists, for instance, developed especially emphatic forms of drawing with powerful delineation and forcible and hyperbolic formal description; notable examples are the works of Ernst Barlach, Käthe Kollwitz, Alfred Kubin, Ernst Ludwig Kirchner, Karl Schmidt-Rottluff, Max Beckmann, and George Grosz. In the artists' group Der Blaue Reiter (The Blue Rider), Wassily Kandinsky was foremost in laying the groundwork for a new evaluation of the nonrepresentational line.

The drawings of the 20th century seem to reflect the restlessness, the motion, and the scientific progress of the age. Some of them are characterized by free line. Others, like those of Fernand Léger, reduce life to geometrical forms (Cubism). X-ray techniques, in which one can see the inside and outside of forms at the same time, have produced drawings unlike those of any other period. Artists who were concerned with expressionism attempted to record the emotional feeling of a scene rather than its realistic appearance. The Surrealists were interested in the subconscious mind and in the interpretation of psychoanalytic problems.

Three 20th-century artists, in particular, found new
ways to communicate ideas. The French artist Henri
Matisse, a master of line, used only essential strokes
and produced drawing that is crisp and uncluttered.
The graphic work of the Swiss-born artist Paul Klee

Henri Matisse sits at an easel drawing with chalk at his home in Nice,
France, in 1948. Matisse used only the most necessary lines to create
his drawings.

combines caricature with the simplicity of children's drawings. Pablo Picasso, a Spanish artist who worked in France for many years, experimented with many different techniques and painted in a great variety of styles during his unusually long career. One technique involves superimposing transparent planes one on top of the other in order to show several sides of an object at the same time. This approach to drawing also makes the subject look like it is rotating slowly.

Into the 21st century, artists continue to use the graphite pencil, for example, as a device for autonomous artworks as well as for sketching and for making preliminary rehearsals of conceptions later carried out in painting or sculpture. Yet the most basic and time-honored tool of the draftsman—the pencil—is in some places yielding to the digital era. Computer graphics, the production of images on computers for use in any medium, is widely used by artists and draftsmen today. Images used in the graphic design of printed material are frequently produced on computers, as are the still and moving images seen in comic strips and animations. The realistic images viewed and manipulated in electronic games and computer simulations could not be created or supported without the enhanced capabilities of modern computer graphics. Computer graphics also are essential to scientific visualization, a discipline that uses images and colours to model complex phenomena such as air currents and electric fields, and to computer-aided engineering and design, in which objects are drawn and analyzed in computer programs. Even the windows-based graphical user interface, now a common means of interacting with innumerable computer programs, is a product of computer graphics. Computer graphics rely heavily on standard software packages. VRML (virtual reality modeling language) is a graphics description language for World Wide Web applications. Today many digital artists use tablets to create their drawings and illustrations onscreen with a technical pen. There are plentiful digital devices and drawing apps available for an artist, both professional and beginner, and they can be tailored to each person's talent and preferences.

People have been drawing since prehistoric times, and early drawings eventually developed into writing. Egyptian writing, hieroglyphics, was a system of picture symbols. The characters in Chinese writing started as drawings. Chinese artists made ink drawings as early as 3,000 years ago. By about 1,000 years ago the Chinese drew on scrolls.

Drawing in Europe became a form of fine art during the Renaissance. The Renaissance was a time of great culture that lasted from the 1300s through the 1500s. Artists in Italy—including Leonardo da Vinci, Raphael, and Michelangelo—made many exquisite drawings. Da Vinci created drawings of the human body as well as scientific drawings. In Germany the artist Albrecht Dürer made detailed pen-and-ink drawings of religious subjects, while later European artists made drawings that showed their opinions. In the 1700s the English artist William Hogarth made drawings that made fun of human mistakes, and in the 1800s the Spanish artist Francisco de Goya made drawings that showed the horrors of war.

In the 1900s many artists made drawings that looked less realistic than earlier drawings—they used geometric shapes or free-flowing lines to represent people and objects. Some artists made abstract drawings, which were meant to express emotions or ideas.

Drawing occupies a considerable place in the work (including all its variants of style and form) of Pablo Picasso, who knew how to make use of its manifold technical possibilities. One is surely justified in calling him the greatest draftsman of the 20th century and one of the greatest in the history of drawing.

Today drawing continues to be a popular form of art. People employ drawing for many business and entertainment purposes, including advertisers who use drawings to sell products. Fashion artists and designers of products make use of drawings to plan their work. Illustrators and cartoonists draw pictures for books, newspapers, and magazines—in print and online. In addition, many children and adults draw just for fun or relaxation because it is still an incredibly vibrant and viable art form.

GLOSSARY

agglutinant An adhesive.

bast A strong, woody fibre obtained chiefly from the phloem of plants and used especially in cordage, matting, and fabrics.

cartoon A design, drawing, or painting made as a model for the finished work.

chiaroscuro Pictorial representation in terms of light and shade without regard to color; the arrangement or treatment of light and dark parts in a pictorial work of art.

convergent Tending to move toward one point or to approach each other.

cross-hatching The engraving or drawing of a series of parallel lines that cross.

Cubist A follower of Cubism, an art form characterized by the abstraction of natural forms into fragmented shapes sometimes organized to depict the subject simultaneously from several points of view.

delineate To indicate by lines drawn in the form or figure of: represent by sketch, design, or diagram; to sketch out or portray.

emulsion A light-sensitive coating on photographic plates, film, or paper consisting of particles of a silver salt suspended in a thick substance (as a gelatin solution).

fascicle One of the divisions of a book published in parts.

fixative A varnish used especially for the protection of pencil or charcoal drawings.

foreshortening The method of rendering a specific object or figure in a picture in depth.

gum Any of numerous complex colloidal substances (as gum arabic) that are exuded by plants or are extracted from them by solvents, that are thick or sticky when moist but harden on drying and are either soluble in water or swell up in contact with water, and that are used in pharmacy (as for emulsifiers), for adhesives, as food thickeners, and in inks.

hatching The engraving or drawing of fine lines close together to give the effect of shading.

iconography The science of identification, description, classification, and interpretation of symbols, themes, and subject matter in the visual arts. Also, an artist's use of this imagery in a particular work.

inimical Harmful.

nonrepresentational art Nonobjective art, also called abstract art, in which the portrayal of things from the visible world plays no part.

orthographic projection Projection of a single view of an object onto a drawing surface in which the lines of projection are perpendicular to the drawing surface.

pentimento (pl. pentimenti) From the Italian *pentirsi*, meaning "to repent," it is the reappearance in an oil painting of original elements of drawing or painting that the artist tried to obliterate by overpainting.

perspective The method of graphically depicting three-dimensional objects and spatial relationships on a two-dimensional plane or on a plane that is shallower than the original.

plethora An excessive quantity or fullness.

realism The theory or practice in art, literature, and theater of showing things as they really are and without idealization.

resin Any of various solid or semisolid fusible natural organic substances that are usually transparent or translucent and yellowish to brown, are formed especially in plant secretions, are soluble in organic solvents but not in water, are electrical nonconductors, and are used chiefly in varnishes, printing inks, plastics, and sizes and in medicine.

sepia A brown pigment from the ink of cuttlefishes.

sinopia A red pigment made from sinopite, a brick-red ferruginous clay that was used by the ancients as a paint. The term is also used to refer to an underdrawing or a preliminary sketch for a monumental work.

tone Colour quality or value: a tint or shade of colour; a colour that modifies another (grey with a blue tone).

Ukiyo-e A Japanese artistic movement from the 17th through the 19th centuries characterized by paintings and colour prints depicting contemporary life and pleasures.

vanishing point A point at which a group of receding parallel lines seems to meet when represented in linear perspective.

vellum A fine-grained lambskin, kidskin, or calfskin prepared especially for writing on or for binding books; a strong cream-coloured paper resembling vellum.

GENERAL WORKS ON DRAWING

Joseph Meder, *The Mastery of Drawing,* trans. and rev. by Winslow Ames, 2 vol. (1978; originally published in German, 1919; 2nd ed., 1923), a voluminous work that remains the basic treatment of the history and techniques of drawing. Arthur E. Popham published an introduction to drawing in *A Handbook to the Drawings and Watercolours in the Department of Prints and Drawings of the British Museum* (1939), based on the ample materials held by the British Museum. Charles De Tolnay in *History and Technique of Old Master Drawings* (1943, reprinted 1972); and James Watrous in *The Craft of Old-Master Drawings* (1957), deal, from different points of view, with the history and techniques of the old masters; while Heribert Hutter in *Drawing: History and Technique* (1968; originally published in German, 1966), stresses the artistic function of drawing and includes modern works. David L. Faber and Daniel Marcus Mendelowitz, *A Guide to Drawing,* 8th ed. (2012), provides a historical résumé, with reference to the artistic elements and technical means of drawing; in the supplement to the 1st ed., *Drawing: A Study Guide* (1967), he offers practical instructions for drawing techniques and their application; as does Robert Beverly Hale in *Drawing Lessons from the Great Masters* (1964, reprinted 1974). Jakob Rosenberg illustrates the possibilities of drawing in *Great Draughtsmen from Pisanello to Picasso,* rev. ed. (1974), with samples from the works of eight great artists. *Great Drawings of All Time,* ed. by Ira Moskowitz and Victoria Thorston, 5 vol. in 6 (1962–79), contains a summary with comments by leading authorities. M.W. Evans, *Medieval Drawings* (1969), is useful for the early history of the art of drawing; Paul J. Sachs, *Modern Prints and Drawings: A Guide to a Better Understanding of Modern Draughtsmanship* (1954), is also useful. Interesting information can be found in catalogs of many exhibitions and collections, such as Bernice Rose, *Drawing Now* (1976). The number of detailed investigations in regard to individual countries, periods, and artists is too large to be listed in this bibliography. One that can be especially recommended, however, is Edward J. Olszewski, *The Draftsman's Eye: Late Italian Renaissance Schools and Styles* (1981).

ART CONSERVATION AND RESTORATION

Valuable general accounts of the field are contained in *Art and Archaeology Technical Abstracts* (semiannual), published by the International Institute for Conservation of Historic and Artistic Work, London. Other general examinations include Andrew Oddy (W.A. Oddy) (ed.), *The Art of the Conservator* (1992); James Beck and Michael Daley, *Art Restoration: The Culture, the Business, and the Scandal* (1993, reprinted 1996); and Nicholas Stanley Price, M. Kirby Talley, Jr., and Alesandra Melucco Vaccaro (eds.), *Historical and Philosophical Issues in the Conservation of Cultural Heritage* (1996). See also John M.A. Thompson et al. (eds.), *The Manual of Curatorship: A Guide to Museum Practice*, 2nd ed. (1992); and Garry Thomson, *The Museum Environment*, 2nd ed. (1986, reprinted 1998). Up-to-the-moment information on specific topics can be found at the Web site for the American Institute for Conservation of Historic and Artistic Works, http://aic.stanford.edu; and the Web site for the International Centre for the Study of the Preservation and Restoration of Cultural Property, http://www.iccrom.org.

Studies of works on paper include Francis W. Dolloff and Roy L. Perkinson, *How to Care for Works of Art on Paper*, 4th ed. (1985); Anne F. Clapp, *Curatorial Care of Works of Art on Paper: Basic Procedures for Paper Preservation*, 3rd rev. ed. (1978, reissued 1987); and Chris Foster, Annette Manick, and Roy L. Perkinson, *Matting and Framing Works of Art on Paper* (1994).

DRAFTING

Aspects of drafting from basic instruction to industrial practices are treated in Walter C. Brown, *Drafting for Industry* (1974, reprinted 1984), a comprehensive treatment including coverage of CAD; Paul Wallach, *Metric Drafting* (1979), with emphasis on the use of the international metric system for dimensioning and tolerancing; and Paul C. Barr *et al., CAD: Principles and Applications* (1985), which covers general-purpose CAD functions and applications to industrial practice and training. William T. Goodban and Jack J.

Hayslett, *Architectural Drawing and Planning,* 3rd ed. (1979), discusses architectural sketching and drafting, including design concepts. See also George E. Rowbotham (ed.), *Engineering and Industrial Graphics Handbook* (1982).

JACQUES CALLOT

Howard Daniel (ed.), *Callot's Etchings* (1974); Gerald Kahan, *Jacques Callot: Artist of the Theatre* (1976).

ALBRECHT DÜRER

Peter Strieder, *The Hidden Dürer* (1978), is a popular biography and introduction to his works. Francis Russell, *The World of Dürer, 1471–1528* (1967, reissued 1981), a vol. in the "Time-Life Library of Art," provides a general introduction to his background, life, and followers. Marcel Brion, *Dürer* (1960), is a critical biography. Heinz Lüdecke, *Albrecht Dürer* (1972), examines Dürer in relation to contemporary social and political concerns. Classic works include Heinrich Wölfflin, *The Art of Albrecht Dürer* (1971; originally published in German, 1905); and Erwin Panofsky, *The Life and Art of Albrecht Dürer,* 4th ed. (1955, reissued 1971). Peter Strieder, *Albrecht Dürer: Paintings, Prints, Drawings* (1982), includes biographical data and covers Dürer's work in all media. Walter Strauss (ed.), *Albrecht Dürer: Woodcuts and Wood Blocks* (1980), is an extensive reference, reproducing all Dürer's work in this medium in chronological order, discussing each at length. Walter Strauss, *The Complete Drawings of Albrecht Dürer,* 6 vol. (1974), is a comprehensive collection, also arranged chronologically, and fully documented. Christopher White, *Dürer: The Artist and His Drawings* (1971), examines Dürer's skill as a draftsman. Walter Koschatzky, *Albrecht Dürer: The Landscape Water-colours* (1973), discusses the 32 surviving landscapes. Fritz Koreny, *Albrecht Dürer and the Animal and Plant Studies of the Renaissance* (1988), illuminates Dürer's genius by comparing his work with contemporary copyists and imitators.

HOKUSAI

J.R. Hillier, *Hokusai: Paintings, Drawings, and Woodcuts* (1955), the best general appreciation of Hokusai in English, though the biographical material is based on outdated sources—includes a detailed listing of his illustrated books; James A. Michener (ed.), *The Hokusai Sketchbooks: Selections from the Manga,* with translations by Richard Lane (1958), a comprehensive sampling of the *Hokusai manga,* with commentary, and translation of all prefaces; Theodore R. Bowie, *The Drawings of Hokusai* (1964), a pioneer study, but flawed by being based largely on forgeries and school copies; Richard Lane, *Masters of the Japanese Print* (1962), includes a critical survey of Hokusai's work and times, based on original sources.

HANS HOLBEIN THE YOUNGER

Exhaustive and still valuable biographies include Alfred Woltmann, *Holbein and His Times* (1872); and Arthur B. Chamberlain, *Hans Holbein the Younger*, 2 vol. (1913). K.T. Parker, *Drawings of Hans Holbein in the Collection of His Majesty the King at Windsor Castle* (1945), is a scholarly account of what is probably the single most important collection of Holbein's mature drawings. Paul Ganz, *The Paintings of Hans Holbein* (1950), is a detailed monograph. John Rowlands, *Holbein: The Paintings of Hans Holbein the Younger* (1985), is complete and up-to-date. Roy Strong, *Holbein and Henry VIII* (1967), examines this important aspect of Holbein's career.

KÄTHE KOLLWITZ

Martha Kearns, *Käthe Kollwitz: Woman and Artist* (1976); Tom Fecht (ed.), *Käthe Kollwitz: Works in Color*, trans. by A.S. Wensinger and R.H. Wood (1988; originally published in German, 1987); Elizabeth Prelinger, Alessandra Comini, and Hildegard Bachert, *Käthe Kollwitz*, exhibition catalog (1992).

LEONARDO DA VINCI

Life and work: Studies of Leonardo's life and work are found in Gabriel Séailles, *Léonard de Vinci, l'artiste & le savant, 1452–1519: essai de biographie psychologique*, new ed., rev. and augmented (1906, reissued 1919); Woldemar von Seidlitz, *Leonardo da Vinci: der Wendepunkt der Renaissance*, definitive ed., edited by Kurt Zoege von Manteuffel (1935), accompanied by extensive documentation; Ludwig Heinrich Heydenreich, *Leonardo da Vinci*, 2 vol. (1954; trans. from new, improved, and enlarged German ed., 1953); Istituto Geografico De Agostini, *Leonardo da Vinci: das Lebensbild eines Genies* (1955; originally published in Italian, 1939), which contains numerous essays and is a richly illustrated compendium of Leonardo's artistic and scientific activity; Morris Philipson (ed.), *Leonardo da Vinci: Aspects of the Renaissance Genius* (1966), which contains valuable contributions to the historical and psychological aspects of Leonardo; V.P. Zubov, *Leonardo da Vinci* (1968, reissued 1996; originally published in Russian, 1961); C.D. O'Malley (ed.), *Leonardo's Legacy: An International Symposium* (1969), a collection of essays exploring various aspects of Leonardo's works; Ritchie Calder, *Leonardo & the Age of the Eye* (1970), which emphasizes his artistic as well as his scientific work; Carlo Pedretti, *Leonardo: A Study in Chronology and Style* (1973, reprinted 1982); Ladislao Reti and Emil M. Bührer (eds.), *The Unknown Leonardo* (1974, reprinted 1990), which contains 10 essays discussing aspects of Leonardo's personality and creativity as made evident in the Madrid Codices; Cecil Gould, *Leonardo: The Artist and the Non-artist* (1975); Robert Payne, *Leonardo* (1978), an account of Leonardo's career, with several new interpretations; Martin Kemp, *Leonardo da Vinci: The Marvellous Works of Nature and Man* (1981, reprinted 1989);

Kenneth Clark, *Leonardo da Vinci*, new ed., rev. by Martin Kemp (1988, reissued 1993); and David Alan Brown, *Leonardo da Vinci: Origins of a Genius* (1998), which examines Leonardo's early career. Angela Ottino della Chiesa (ed.), *The Complete Paintings of Leonardo da Vinci* (1967, reissued 1985; originally published in Italian, 1967), catalogs the paintings, as does Pietro C. Marani, *Leonardo da Vinci: The Complete Paintings* (2000; originally published in Italian, 1999). The standard publication on the drawings is Kenneth Clark, *The Drawings of Leonardo da Vinci in the Collection of Her Majesty the Queen at Windsor Castle*, 2nd ed., rev. with Carlo Pedretti, 3 vol. (1968); a more recent study can be found in Martin Clayton, *Leonardo da Vinci: A Singular Vision* (1996). A.E. Popham (ed.), *The Drawings of Leonardo da Vinci*, 2nd ed. (1947, reissued 1973), is also important for the study of Leonardo as a draftsman.

The notebooks: Augusto Marinoni, "I manoscritti di Leonardo da Vinci e le loro edizioni," in Comitato Nazionale per le onoranze a Leonardo da Vinci nel quinto centenario della nascita, *Leonardo: Saggi e richerche*, ed. by Achille Marazza (1954), pp. 229–274, is a concise summary of all manuscripts, their facsimile editions, and their chronology and contains other excellent essays by various authors on Leonardo as artist and scientist. Ladislao Reti (ed.), *The Madrid Codices*, 5 vol. (1974), contains facsimiles of the codices (vol. 1–2), commentary by Reti (vol. 3), and Reti's transcription and translation of the codices into English (vol. 4–5). Also of interest are Ladislao Reti, "The Two Unpublished Manuscripts of Leonardo Da Vinci in the Biblioteca Nacional of Madrid—I," *The Burlington Magazine*, 110(778):10–22 (January 1968), and "The Two Unpublished Manuscripts of Leonardo da Vinci in the Biblioteca Nacional of Madrid—II," *The Burlington Magazine*, 110(779):81–89 (February 1968). A. Philip McMahon (trans.), *Treatise on Painting*, 2 vol. (1956), is a facsimile edition of *Codex Urbinas latinus 1270* accompanied by an English translation. Kenneth D. Keele and Carlo Pedretti, *Leonardo da Vinci: Corpus of the Anatomical Studies in the Collection of Her Majesty the Queen at Windsor Castle*, 3 vol. (1978–80), includes a volume of facsimile plates. The best anthologies of Leonardo's literary heritage are Edward MacCurdy (Edward McCurdy) (ed. and trans.), *The Notebooks of Leonardo da Vinci*, 2nd ed., 2 vol. (1955, reissued 1977); and Jean Paul Richter (compiler and ed.), *The Literary Works of Leonardo da Vinci*, 3rd ed., 2 vol., trans. from Italian (1970, reissued 1977). Martin Kemp (ed. and trans.) and Margaret Walker (trans.), *Leonardo on Painting: An Anthology of Writings*, trans. from Italian (1989), is a readable and organized translated collection of Leonardo's notes on art.

CLAUDE LORRAIN

Marcel Röthlisberger, *Claude Lorrain: The Paintings,* 2 vol. (1961, reprinted 1979), and *Claude Lorrain: The Drawings,* 2 vol. (1968), two fully illustrated, complete catalogs, with introductions and notes, are the standard works. They include in English translation all the early material on the artist, including several early biographies. Only the etchings are not adequately covered by Röthlisberger; for these see Lino Mannocci, *The Etchings of Claude Lorrain* (1988). Other recent works include Marco Chiarini (ed.), *Claude Lorrain: Selected Drawings* (1968), with superb plates; Michael Kitson, *The Art of Claude Lorrain* (1969), an exhibition catalog, and *Claude Lorrain, Liber veritatis* (1978), a study of the sketchbook; H. Diane Russell, *Claude Lorrain, 1600–1682* (1982), an exhibition catalog including extensive scholarly essays; and Helen Langdon, *Claude Lorrain* (1989), a synthesis of recent research on the artist.

GIOVANNI BATTISTA PIRANESI

A. Hyatt Mayor, *Giovanni Battista Piranesi* (1952), is a biography. John Wilton-Ely, *The Mind and Art of Giovanni Battista Piranesi* (1978, reissued 1988), *Piranesi as Architect and Designer* (1993), and *Giovanni Battista Piranesi: The Complete Etchings*, 2 vol. (1994), examine the many aspects of Piranesi as a man and as an artist. Mario Bevilacqua, Heather Hyde Minor, and Fabio Barry (eds.), *The Serpent and the Stylus: Essays on G.B. Piranesi* (2006), also examines many aspects of Piranesi's life and work.

LOUIS SULLIVAN

Hugh Morrison, *Louis Sullivan: Prophet of Modern Architecture* (1935, reprinted 1971), is the standard biography, which also includes an evaluation of Sullivan's work. Willard Connely, *Louis Sullivan As He Lived: The Shaping of American Architecture* (1960), is a more personal account, although the full story of his later years will probably never be known.

A

Alberti, Leon Battista, 11–12, 131

Altdorfer, Albrecht, 111, 112, 123, 138

Apocalypse, 35

Apocalypse of St. John, The, 117

architectural drawings, 81–89
  artistic, 121–123

art conservation, 77–80

artistic architectural drawing, 121–123

art restoration, 77–80

At the Concert Européen, 39–40

Audubon, John James, 90–93

B

Barlach, Ernst, 21, 157

Bellini, Jacopo, 30–31, 110, 126, 127–128

Bernini, Gian Lorenzo, 95, 123

bistre, 52, 54–55

Bonnard, Pierre, 29, 45

Borromini, Francesco, 123

Bosch, Hieronymus, 117

Botticelli, Sandro, 31, 62, 93

Boucher, François, 27, 45, 102, 144

Bruegel, Pieter, 111, 117–118, 140

Brunelleschi, Filippo, 11

brush drawings, 61–65

brushwork, 8

Busch, Wilhelm, 95

C

Callot, Jacques, 118, 140, 141–142

camera obscura, 74–75

caricature, 95

cartographic drawings, 89

cartoons, 95–98

Cartoons for the Cause, 119

Cassatt, Mary, 45

Cézanne, Paul, 12, 43, 72, 114, 148

chalks, 18, 24–29

charcoal, 18, 20–21

Chardin, Jean-Baptiste, 29, 45, 102

chiaroscuro, 8

Chodowiecki, Daniel, 93

Clouet, François, 45, 100, 138

Clouet, Jean, 27, 45, 100, 138

coloured crayons, 44

computer graphics, 159–160

Constable, John, 7, 65

Conté, Nicolas-Jacques, 39, 41

Corot, Jean-Baptiste-Camille, 114

Cozens, Alexander, 55, 65, 114

Cranach, Lucas, 105, 112
Crane, Walter, 118–120
croquis, 6
cross-hatching, 7
Cubism, 12, 157

D

Danube School, 111, 112–113, 138
Daumier, Honoré, 93, 148
Dead Christ in the Tomb, 107
Death, 24
Degas, Edgar, 21, 29, 43, 45, 148
Delacroix, Eugène, 43, 65, 148
Dürer, Albrecht, 7, 31, 32–38, 57, 93, 95, 100, 105, 111, 140, 160
Dyck, Anthony Van, 141

E

Eakins, Thomas, 148
Ernst, Max, 40
Expressionists, 5, 24, 29, 49. 115, 157
Eyck, Jan van, 100

F

Family of Burgomaster Meyer Adoring the Virgin, 107
fanciful and nonrepresentational drawings, 117–121

figure compositions and still lifes, 114–115
finger painting, 47
Fragonard, Jean-Honoré, 64, 144
Francesca, Piero della, 131
Frog Prince, The, 119
Fuseli, Henry, 118

G

gallnut ink, 49–52
Géométrie descriptive, 84
Goya, Francisco, 65, 117, 145, 160
graphite point, 39–40
Great Passion, 35

H

hatching, 5–7
cross-hatching, 7
Hirschfeld, Al, 95, 96–97
Hogarth, William, 160
Hokusai, 150–155
Holbein, Hans, the Younger, 27, 45, 100, 103–109, 138
Huber, Wolf, 111, 113, 138

I

illustrations, 93–95
illustrative drawings
caricature, 95
cartoons, 95–98
illustrations, 93–95

incised drawing, 46
India ink, 52–53
Ingres, Jean-Auguste-
    Dominique, 5, 42, 102,
    145
inks, 49–54
In the Dream, 116

J

Jordaens, Jacob, 141

K

Kandinsky, Wassily, 58, 157
Kirchner, Ernst Ludwig, 29,
    157
Klee, Paul, 45, 158
Klimt, Gustav, 44
Klinger, Max, 22
Kollwitz, Käthe, 21, 22–24,
    157
Kubin, Alfred, 95, 157

L

Lady of Shalott, The, 119
Lancret, Nicolas, 27
landscapes, 110–114
*Landscape with Cattle and
    Peasants*, 67
Leonardo da Vinci, 26, 57, 62,
    95, 123, 130–137, 160
Liber Veritatis, 68
Liotard, Jean-Étienne, 27, 45
Lorrain, Claude, 55, 64,
    66–69, 71, 73, 111, 143

M

Manet, Édouard, 21
Masaccio, 11, 127
Matisse, Henri, 51, 58, 116,
    148, 158
mechanical devices, 73–77
metal pens, 50–51
metalpoints, 30–31
Michelangelo, 7, 57, 123,
    129, 138, 160
Miró, Joan, 45
Modigliani, Amedeo, 148
Monge, Gaspard, 84
Moore, Henry, 29, 51, 73
Moreau, Gustave, 29, 45,
    118
Munch, Edvard, 29

N

Nast, Thomas, 95
Neoclassicism, 2, 39, 58,
    102, 114, 122, 145, 148
New York Times, 96
Nolde, Emil, 115

P

pantograph, 82–83
paper manufacturing, 15–17,
    150
pastel, 44–45
Peasants' War, 22
pencil drawing, 40–43
pen drawings, 56–61
pens, 18, 47–49

quill, reed, and metal pens, 50–51
Perry, James, 51
perspective, explanation of, 9–12
Picasso, Pablo, 31, 44, 51, 58, 60–61, 148, 159, 161
Picasso Museum, 60–61
Piranesi, Giovanni Battista, 113, 118, 122–123, 145
Pisanello, Antonio, 56, 100, 126
plane techniques, 8–12
pochade, 6
Portail, Jacques-André, 27
Portrait of a Lady, 21
portraits, 21, 100–103
Potter, Paulus, 21, 143
Poussin, Nicolas, 71, 111, 143

Q

quill pens, 50–51

R

Raphael, 5, 37, 57, 129, 138, 160
Redon, Odilon, 29, 45, 115, 116–117
reed pens, 50–51
Rembrandt, 5, 49, 50, 55, 57, 71, 113, 143, 145
Renaissance, 2, 5, 9, 10, 12, 32, 34, 35, 36, 37, 40, 46, 47, 49, 55, 56, 58, 76, 123, 126, 127, 128, 130, 138, 156, 160
Renoir, Auguste, 45
Robert, Hubert, 144
Rothenberg, Susan, 21
Rowlandson, Thomas, 145, 146–147
Rubens, Peter Paul, 27, 141

S

Saint-Aubin, Gabriel de, 144
Schongauer, Martin, 138
scientific illustrations, 89–90
scratchboard, 94–95
Seghers, Hercules, 143
sepia, 53–54, 54–55
Seurat, Georges, 3, 39, 148
sketches, 6–7
St. Jerome Curing the Lion, 32
Sullivan, Louis, 86–89
surfaces, drawing, 12–13, 15–17
Surrealists, 40, 116, 118, 157

T

Tang dynasty, 149
technical drawings
  architectural drawings, 81–89
  cartographic drawings, 89
  pantograph, 82–83
  scientific illustrations, 89–90
  topographic drawings, 89

Thirty-six Views of Mount Fuji,
    150–151, 155
Tintoretto, Jacopo, 3, 20, 21,
    140
Titian, 57
topographic drawings, 89
Toulouse-Lautrec, Henri de,
    21, 45, 148
Turner, J.M.W., 65, 114

V

van Gogh, Vincent, 5, 43, 49,
    50, 114, 148
Vermeer, Johannes, 74
Vuillard, Jean-Édouard, 29,
    45

W

wash drawing, 62
Watteau, Antoine, 27, 144
Weavers' Revolt, 22
Wei dynasty, 149